a Vision book (repeated pattern)

D1264475

MORE
Champions in Sports and Spirit

Books by ED FITZGERALD

The Turning Point

College Slugger

Yankee Rookie

Player-Manager (with Lou Boudreau)

Champions in Sports and Spirit

I Always Wanted to Be Somebody
   (with Althea Gibson)

More Champions in Sports and Spirit

MORE CHAMPIONS IN SPORTS AND SPIRIT

by

Ed Fitzgerald

illustrated by H. LAWRENCE HOFFMAN

VISION BOOKS

Farrar, Straus & Cudahy   New York
Burns & Oates   London

COPYRIGHT © 1959 BY ED FITZGERALD
LIBRARY OF CONGRESS CATALOG CARD
NUMBER 59–10191

Third Printing, 1962

VISION BOOKS
IS A DIVISION OF
FARRAR, STRAUS & CUDAHY, INC.
PUBLISHED SIMULTANEOUSLY IN CANADA BY
AMBASSADOR BOOKS, LTD., TORONTO.
MANUFACTURED IN THE U.S.A.

Nihil Obstat:
Rt. Rev. Msgr. Peter B. O'Connor
Censor Librorum

Imprimatur:
✠ Most Reverend Thomas A. Boland, S.T.D.
Archbishop of Newark

CONTENTS

Chapter One

STAN MUSIAL, THE NO. 1 BALLPLAYER

Ask a group of fans who has been the greatest hitter in modern baseball, and you are bound to start an argument. Some will say Stan Musial and some will say Ted Williams; others will pick Mickey Mantle or Willie Mays. But ask the same group who is the finest man in the game, the man whose example and character they would most like their own sons to follow, and there will be no argument at all. Every one will give you the name of Stanley Frank

Musial, the pride of the St. Louis Cardinals and, for that matter, of all baseball.

Stan Musial will be ranked as one of the greatest hitters ever to play major-league ball. When he hit .351 for the 1957 season, he won the National League batting championship for the seventh time in his distinguished career. He is one of the handful of super-stars to make more than 3,000 base hits. His lifetime batting average is a spectacular .340 for sixteen seasons. Once, on May 2, 1954, he hit five home runs in one afternoon, in a double-header. He is a fixture on the National League All-Star team, and when the *Sporting News*, baseball's newspaper, polled the baseball writers in 1956 to select the Player of the Decade (from 1946 to 1956), the man who won out over such competition as Joe DiMaggio and Bob Feller and Ted Williams was Stan Musial. The simple listing of his batting feats takes up hundreds of lines in the baseball record books.

But the biggest thing about Stan Musial in the minds of the millions of Americans who follow the game closely is that he is a wonderful man. His good nature, his kindness, his clean speech and courteous manner, his amazing modesty in the face of all the adulation that has come his way, are the things one thinks of first in connection with him. Certainly he is a great ballplayer, but a great human being, too.

There are all kinds of stories about Stan that help throw some light on the kind of man he is.

When Stan was a rookie pitcher at Daytona Beach in the Florida State League in 1940, his manager was Dickie Kerr, who earned a place in baseball history by pitching two victories for the Chicago White Sox in the World Series of 1919. That was the Series which the stars of the Sox later admitted they were paid to lose. Kerr was fond of the tall, slim young Polish boy from the coal-mining town of Donora, Pennsylvania. Even after Stan hurt his shoulder tumbling while making a catch in the outfield and couldn't continue pitching, Kerr encouraged him to stay in the game. He insisted that Stan could make the big league on his batting alone. Even then Musial looked like a hitter.

On the personal side, too, Kerr was sympathetic to Stan and his young wife, Lillian, who had been his high school sweetheart. Mr. and Mrs. Kerr invited the young couple, who were a thousand miles from their families in Donora, to live with them until after the birth of their first child. Lillian and Stan never forgot the kindness of Dickie Kerr and his wife. They named their child Richard and called him Dick. Eighteen years later, in the spring of 1958, they tried to express their appreciation in a more practical fashion by buying the Kerrs, then in their sixties, a comfortable new home in Daytona Beach, where they are living in retirement. Stan didn't mention the incident to anyone, and the extraordinarily generous gift would have gone unnoticed if a Florida newspaperman hadn't heard about it and broken the story to the world. All over the United States, people reading about it in their morning papers nodded their heads and said to themselves, "That's Stan Musial for you. It's just like him to do something like that and never say a word about it."

Dickie Kerr tells another revealing story about Musial, dating back to that 1940 season in Daytona Beach when Stan was a struggling rookie trying to get along on a season's salary of less money ($100 a month for five months) than he is paid today for a single game (approximately $700, based on his salary of $100,000 for a season of 154 games). "We had a few wild kids on the ball club," Kerr says, "and I used to have to watch some of them pretty closely. Sometimes I'd even stay up late at night to catch them coming in from a party or a date, and I'd lecture them about the importance of getting their sleep. I never had to say anything to Musial, though. He was about as serious as any young ballplayer I ever saw; he was all business. So you can imagine how surprised I was when I walked out of the hotel one Sunday morning at about 6:30 and saw Stan walking down the street toward me, all dressed up. I said to him, 'Stan, I'm surprised at you, staying out all night. Where've you been?' And I was pretty embarrassed when he laughed and said, 'Out all night? Not me, Skip. I just came from six o'clock Mass.'"

Bill Corum, the famous sportswriter, said, "Once, with great reluctance, because I hated to impose on him, I asked Stan to appear at a sports dinner in my home town, which is about 180 miles from St. Louis. It was wintertime, and the night was mean and cold. The roads were slick and dangerous. But Stan drove his own car the round trip of 360 miles, ate the customary rubber chicken, made the small dinner a great big success, and just brushed it off when I tried to thank him and tell him how much I appreciated it."

A veteran ballplayer, Hank Sauer, has played both with and against Stan. In a talk with writer Roger Kahn about Stan's affection for children, Hank said, "Whenever we were in St. Louis, he'd always be holding open house. He has a tremendous family. I mean they're nice, his wife and the three kids, Dick, Gerry, and Janet. He's got the nicest family and home and wife you've ever seen. If your kids rip up something at his house, and you start to give them the dickens for it, he'll chew you out. 'Never mind what they do,' he'll say, 'let them alone. They're at my house and they can do anything they want.'

"Whenever you go to his house, you fall all over kids. They're all over the place. 'That's what my home is for,' I heard him say once. 'It's for kids, yours and mine.'"

Back in 1946, the top stars of the game were being tempted by lavish money offers to turn their backs on the U.S. major leagues and sign up to play in the Mexican League. A wealthy Mexico City businessman, Jorge Pasquel, was pouring money into a campaign to make the league a big-time operation, and he realized that

the quickest and best way to achieve his goal
was to lure a half dozen or so of the biggest stars
south of the border. Pasquel visited the Musials
at their St. Louis apartment early in 1946 and,
in a carefully planned, theatrical gesture, opened
a briefcase and spilled $75,000 in greenbacks
on the kitchen table. He offered Stan the whole
pile as a bonus for signing a Mexican League
contract. In addition, Stan would get $125,000
in salary payments to be spread over five years.
This meant that Musial, who was being paid
$15,000 a year by the Cardinals, could earn
$200,000, or an average of $40,000 a year, for
five years of baseball in Mexico.

It was a great deal of money to the boy
from Donora. It would mean financial inde-
pendence for his family. With $75,000 in the
bank, he would probably never have to worry
about money again, even if he was hurt and
unable to continue his career. But it would
mean something else, too; it would mean that
he had run out on the contract he had signed
with the Cardinals to play ball for them through
the season of 1946. Eddie Dyer, who was
managing the Cards then, saw Stan's preoccupa-
tion with this side of the problem and ham-
mered the point hard. "Do you," he asked,

"want to be known as a man whose word is no good?" Stan didn't. He said a polite no, thanks, to Pasquel and stayed in the uniform of the Redbirds. It is unlikely that he ever will wear any other.

The boy who grew up to become an American hero was born on November 21, 1920, in Donora, the son of Lukasz Musial, a Polish immigrant small in stature but wiry and strong, and Mary Lancos Musial, a sturdy New York girl of Czech descent. Stan was their first child. His father, until the day he died, called him Stashu.

"He was always the nice boy he is now," his mother told a reporter last year. "He never sassed anybody. Ask his teachers. And his head is still the same, it's got no bigger, but now he speaks a lot better than he used to."

As soon as Stanley was old enough, his father began taking him to the Polish National Alliance hall in Donora for tumbling workouts. The Poles, like many of the Middle European peoples, are enthusiastic gymnasts, and Lukasz Musial was a firm believer in the old-fashioned principle of a sound mind in a sound body. Stan enjoyed the exercise, up to a point. The point was reached when the neighborhood kids

introduced him to the American game of baseball. He took to it immediately, and that was
the end of his weekly tumbling drills. Once
Stan began playing baseball, his father had to
make the trips to the Polish National Alliance
alone.

In school, Stan was a good student if not an
outstanding one. Urged on by his father, who
had had to work with his hands all of his life
and was obsessed by the determination that his
son would do better, he applied himself suffi-
ciently to keep his marks well above passing.
Stan was so serious about school that during his
third year in high school he improved his credits
by going back to junior high for one period a
day to take algebra, a subject he had skipped
during his own junior high years. He thought
he might need it some day, and even though he
had to take the class with a group much
younger than himself, he made up his mind to
go through with it. "Most boys," one of his
teachers has said, "would not have risked the
ridicule of their friends. It was the measure of
Stan's character that he dared to be different."

At Donora High School, Stan, already almost
six feet tall, was a star baseball and basketball
player. In baseball, he was a pitcher, but he

was such a good hitter that he played the out-field whenever he wasn't pitching. In basketball, he was the master of a left-handed hook shot that made him one of the most consistent scorers on the team. His occasional experiments with football convinced everyone in school that he would be a fine football player too, but his father, suspicious of the game that he had heard caused so many injuries, refused to allow him to play.

Lukasz Musial was soon drawn into a prominent role in his son's athletic career. Stan wanted to play professional baseball and his father wanted him to go to college. Because of his insistence on a college education for the boy, Mr. Musial was inclined to view basketball in a favorable light because it was soon clear to him that the goal of all the good basketball players in town was a college scholarship. This struck him as a lot more sensible than signing a baseball contract and going off to play for a little town in West Virginia or Ohio for sixty-five dollars a month.

But Stan was stubborn. He didn't want to go to college and play basketball. He loved baseball and he thought he might be good enough to make a living at it. Anyway, he wanted to try. So he argued and argued and argued with his father, and finally, much against his will and certainly against his better judgment, Lukasz gave in. Not all at once, though, not quickly or easily.

Stan, who was going steady with Lillian Labash, the daughter of the man who owned the grocery store on the corner, had both Lillian and Helen Kloz, the high school librarian, in his corner. "If your heart is in baseball," Miss Kloz told him, "it seems to me you ought to follow it at least for a while and see how you make out." Then, during his last year in high school, he picked up two more persuasive advocates. Andy French, the business manager of the Cardinals' Pennsylvania State League farm club at Monessen, across the river from Donora, and Ollie Vanek, the Monessen manager, became greatly interested in him. French saw him pitch a few games for Donora High and invited him to work out with the Monessen club so that Vanek could look him over. Stan did, several times, and Vanek was impressed, not so much with his pitching as with his hitting.

Toward the end of the school year, the two baseball men made several visits to the Musial home in an effort to get Stan's signature—and

Lukasz's too, because Stan was a minor—on a contract. They had no luck until one day, as they went over the same old arguments, Stan's mother, who was sitting in a corner of the living room, noticed that Stan was crying quietly. For the first time since the discussions had been going on, she spoke up. "Lukasz," she said, "look, he's crying. You ought to be ashamed making Stanley feel so bad. He's a good boy. If he wants to play the baseball, if it makes him happy, let him do it."

Lukasz Musial, the head of the house, the man who hated working in the mill and wanted to be sure his son never had to do it, was defeated. He nodded soberly. "All right," he said, "all right. Go play, Stanley. I sign. I'm sorry I make you feel bad."

Stanley went and played. He didn't exactly set the world on fire, but he did all right. In his first season at Williamson, West Virginia, in the Mountain State League, he won six games and lost six. He did a little better in his second year, with the same club, winning nine and losing only two. More important, although nobody was aware of it at the time, was the fact that he raised his batting average from .258 to .352.

At the end of the year, on his nineteenth birthday, November 21, 1939, he eloped with Lillian Labash. They didn't say anything about it to either of their families until the winter was almost over; they were afraid that Lukasz Musial would object to their getting married on $65 a month. In the spring, though, when the Cardinals ordered Stan to report to Daytona Beach, Lillian went with him. They were determined to test the old saying that two can live as cheaply as one. In their case, they didn't have much choice; two were going to have to live as cheaply as one.

The best news the Musials got after little Dickie was born was the word that the Cardinals were going to promote Stan to a ball club in a higher classification, in spite of his damaging shoulder injury. Maybe it was because his pitching record of eighteen victories and only five defeats looked good enough to take a chance on. Maybe it was because his batting average, a robust .311 with 70 runs-batted-in, made him look like an all-round ballplayer. Anyway, the big club was interested in him. The trouble was, the minor-league managers weren't. All of the Cards' top farm teams refused to take him on.

It was a discouraging experience. Stan reported that spring to a vast encampment for class B, C and D ballplayers that the Cardinals maintained at Columbus, Georgia. There he worked to try to attract the attention of any manager who might be willing to take a chance on a sore-armed pitcher with some potential as an outfielder and hitter. One day, while he was shagging flies on one of the numerous diamonds, he spotted his old friend from Monessen, Ollie Vanek. Stan knew that Vanek was going to manage the Springfield club in the class C Western Association that year, and impulsively he ran up to him. "Mr. Vanek," he began politely, "can I speak to you for a minute?"

"Sure, kid," Vanek said amiably. "What's on your mind?"

"You remember me, don't you?" Stan asked hopefully.

The manager wrinkled his forehead. "I know you from some place," he said, "but I can't remember where."

"Stan Musial. From Donora. Remember?"

"Oh, sure. You've filled out a lot. You look different. Who are you with?"

"Last year I was with Daytona in D," Stan said.

"That's right. I heard something about you around the office."

It was now or never. Stan took a deep breath and then plunged in. "Mr. Vanek," he said quickly, "will you give me a chance with your ball club? I think I can help you." He waited, tense and scared. Vanek looked him over carefully. "All right, kid," he said finally. "I will."

Vanek wasn't sure what he could do with Stan, but there would be no harm in seeing what the boy could do as an outfielder. He looked good in the batting cage, and his record suggested that he might be a hitter. Ollie protected himself by exacting from the front office a promise that he would get another pitcher as soon as one was available, and he gave Stan a trial in right field. By the time spring training was over, Stan was hitting steadily and Vanek was sure the experiment was going to succeed. The only question was Stan's throwing arm, still very weak from the crippling effects of the injury at Daytona Beach.

"I noticed," Vanek remembered years later, "that he would try to charge in much too fast on ground balls hit to him in the outfield. What he was trying to do, of course, was shorten the throws he'd have to make. He also had a little trouble fielding line drives. But his few weaknesses didn't last very long. I've never seen a young ballplayer work as hard as Stan did. He'd get out there early every morning and practice shagging flies in the outfield. In fact, he was the only ballplayer on the club who would come to me and ask me to give him extra fielding practice. Most ballplayers, you know, like to take all the batting practice they can get, but they regard the other stuff as manual labor. Not Stan. He couldn't get enough of it."

The rookie's hard work paid off. When the regular Western Association season started in Springfield, Stan had his eye on the ball, and his slender, wiry body was in perfect shape. He stayed in the starting lineup every day and whaled the cover off the ball. At the end of the first month his batting average was a fantastic .440, and although he tailed off somewhat after that, he still was hitting .379 when late in July Branch Rickey, the general manager of the Cardinals, put through a long-distance telephone call to Vanek.

"Is Musial ready for double-A ball?" Rickey asked. "We could use him in Rochester."

"He certainly is," Vanek said. "Except for his throwing arm, which is still a little weak, this boy is ready for anything."

"Good," Rickey said. "I'll come down tomorrow and take a look at him."

Vanek didn't tell Stan that the big boss was coming. He thought it might upset him and make him press too hard. The strategy paid off handsomely. With Mr. Rickey sitting unobtrusively in the grandstand, Stan slugged a home run and a triple and found himself, a few hours later, promoted to the Rochester Red Wings of the International League, then widely regarded as the top minor league in the country.

It represented a big jump for the youngster, from class C baseball to double-A, but Stan wasted no time dispelling any doubts about his ability to make the grade. On his first time at bat for the Red Wings, he hit a booming home run. From then on, it was clear that to him the pitchers in this league were no different from the pitchers in the Western Association. He belted them for a .326 batting average before the Cardinals summoned him again, in September.

There was no place to go this time but to the big league itself, to Sportsman's Park in St.

Louis, the home of the mighty Cardinals, and that's where Stan went, dazed but happy, nervous but confident. He got into a dozen ball games, every one of them a pressure-packed battle because the Cards were fighting the Brooklyn Dodgers desperately for the National League pennant. He batted an electric .426.

Nobody knew who he was, or even how to pronounce his name, when he first put on a Cardinal uniform that summer. But when the season was over, they knew all about him. "Everything," sportswriter Tom Meany said, "except how to pitch to him." That's the one thing they still haven't found out.

An oddity of Musial's flying progress that season from a sore-armed class C pitcher to a slugging major-league outfielder is the fact that he posted the highest batting average recorded that year in each of the three leagues in which he played. But, because he didn't stay long enough in any one of the three to qualify, he didn't win the batting championship of any one. That was a trifling point, however. He was in the big league, a member of the St. Louis Cardinals with those dashing redbirds on his chest and a big number six on his back, and he was the happiest man in the world.

Stan's tremendous value to the Cardinals is best illustrated by the fact that, beginning with 1942, his first full season, St. Louis won the pennant three years in a row. He hit .315 in 1942, won his first National League batting championship with a .357 average in 1943 (and, incidentally, was named the league's Most Valuable Player), and came right back with a highly respectable .347 in 1944. Sam Breadon, who owned the Cardinals then, told reporters that the best day's work he had ever done for the ball club was saying no to an offer of $40,000 the New York Giants made for Musial when he was still with Springfield early in 1941. "I couldn't see the idea of selling Stan," Breadon said. "I felt a hitter like that belonged on the Cardinals."

Through the years, the various owners of the St. Louis club have had many opportunities to sell Musial's contract or to trade him for a flock of other players and a large amount of cash to boot. They always have refused. It's unlikely that they even gave the offers a second thought, although it must be hard not to give a second thought to some of the enormous sums that have been mentioned in connection with obtaining Stan's services. The Cardinals without

Musial would be like Sunday dinner without a roast. Stan *is* the Cardinals. Even in retirement, whether or not he ever manages the ball club, he undoubtedly will be a part of the organization, the living symbol of St. Louis baseball.

Not only St. Louis but the whole population that follows baseball will never forget Musial's spectacular record: the day he hit those five home runs in a double-header against the Giants; the year he destroyed Brooklyn's pitching staff by compiling an awesome .545 batting average for his season's work at Ebbets Field, thus inspiring the shocked but admiring Brooklyn fans to give him the majestically simple nickname, "The Man"; the day at Chicago in May, 1958, when Stan pinch-hit a dramatic double for the 3,000th base hit of his career and joined seven other baseball immortals in the ultra-exclusive 3,000-hit club. Only Ty Cobb, Honus Wagner, Paul Waner, Tris Speaker, Eddie Collins, Napoleon Lajoie and Pop Anson were able to achieve that goal before Musial reached it in his sixteenth season.

"He is a legend in his own time," Dick Meyer of the Cardinals' front office said at a dinner given in his honor a few weeks after he had struck the momentous blow. It was no exaggeration. Stan has been such a magnificent player for so many years that people can seriously refer to a season like the one he had in 1947, when he hit .312, with nineteen home runs and ninety-five runs-batted-in, as a bad year. It is a measure of Musial's greatness as a batsman that in the twelve seasons from 1946 through 1957, he failed only twice to drive in at least 100 runs. The highest batting average he has ever posted in a full season was the .376 he hit in 1948, but the fact that he has averaged .340 over his entire career shows his remarkable consistency.

The records prove amply that there is nothing lucky about Stan's hitting. As modest as he is, he recognizes this himself and is willing to discuss his gift objectively. By his own evaluation, the cornerstone of the whole thing is his ability to tell almost as soon as the ball leaves the pitcher's hand what the pitch is going to be. "I can tell by the speed," he has admitted. "Every pitcher has a set of speeds. I mean, the curve goes one speed and the slider goes at something else. Well, if I concentrate, I can pick up the speed of the ball about the first thirty feet it travels. When I concentrate, halfway in I know what the pitch is going to be and how the ball is going to move when it gets up to home plate."

Yogi Berra, the star home-run hitter of the Yankees, was asked if he thought it was possible to do this. "Sure," he said after giving the proposition long thought. "It's possible. Most guys couldn't do it. I don't do it. But that guy could"—which is as good a testimonial to Stan Musial's genius as any.

Another scrupulously honest judgment is that of Johnny Antonelli, the number one pitcher of the San Francisco Giants. Asked how it was best to pitch to Musial, Antonelli said, "Well, I've heard you should throw him fast balls, and I've heard you should curve him, and throw him the change-up. I figure I have to go fast with him. It's my best pitch, and you have to go against Musial with your best. . . . Me, all the guys around the league, we try to get him out with our best."

Perhaps the clearest insight of all into Musial's hitting is provided by one of his own recollections. "Harry Brecheen (a former St. Louis pitcher) was sitting in the stands the other day," he said. "I got two hits the first two times up, and Harry told me after the game that I didn't seem to be bearing down as much after I got those hits. He's right. You get a couple of hits the first few times up like that and you take it for granted. I can almost feel myself letting up. The really big average is a matter of concentration. You've got to concentrate on every pitch." At that time Stan's batting average was a ferocious .467.

Another indication of Stan's modesty in connection with his own batting skill is his persistent refusal, despite the more than 400 home runs to his credit, to think of himself as a slugger. "I'm just a little old singles hitter," he says. "Besides, I prefer four singles to one homer any day in the week. I don't mean to say I'll refuse the home-run championship if I should win it some time, but I certainly have no intention of trying for it. When I try for the long ball, I never hit a homer. I hit thirty-nine home runs in 1948 without consciously trying to hit even one. So I began to wonder what I'd be able to do if I really tried, and the next year I deliberately went for the fences. Well, I not only stopped hitting home runs, I also stopped hitting singles. That's when I quit being a slugger. I haven't tried for a home run since."

As soon as he had said that, Stan held up his

hand like a traffic cop. "I forgot," he said sheep-
ishly. "I did try when I hit my fifth home run
in that 1954 double-header against the Giants.
After I'd hit the fourth one, the public address
announcer said I'd just tied the record for the
most home runs in a single day. Up to then I
hadn't paid any attention to the homers. I'd
just met the ball solidly four times and it had
gone all the way. But then I really wanted
another one. Hoyt Wilhelm was pitching for
the Giants and I'd never hit him very well. He
threw me one of those knucklers of his, and,
boy, that fifth homer was the best shot of them
all. It went all the way over the roof in right
center."

Stan finished his story characteristically.
"When I got home that night," he said, "my
boy Dickie, who was twelve then, met me at
the door and said, 'Gee, Dad, those guys must
have thrown you a lot of fat pitches today.'"

Dickie, who is a big boy now and a student
at the University of Notre Dame, is also re-
sponsible for one of the most accurate appraisals
of his father ever to get into print. He de-
livered it when he was eight years old.

"Did you know that my father used to be

a pitcher?" Dickie asked a reporter visiting the house.

"I've heard that he was," the reporter said.

"He was a pretty good pitcher," Dickie said. "He can also play first base, and I guess you know he plays the outfield." The little boy was thoughtful for a moment. "Do you know my father very well?" he asked, finally.

"No," the reporter said. "Tell me about him."

"I like him," Dickie said. "He's a nice guy."

And that's as good a way as any to tell what Stan Musial is like.

Chapter Two

CARMEN BASILIO, EVERYBODY'S FAVORITE FIGHTER

When many boxing fans think of Carmen Basilio, the determined fighter from Chittenango, New York, who has held both the welterweight and middleweight championships of the world, they think right away of a stern-faced gladiator kneeling in the center of the ring after the bell has sounded to end the last round. As the shouts of excited thousands beat down around his head, he solemnly makes the sign of the cross.

Like many of the great boxing champions who have occupied the center of the stage before him, men like Jack Dempsey, Gene Tunney, Joe Louis and Rocky Marciano, Carmen is at heart a man of peace. He rarely argues with anybody and he almost never raises his voice. Despite the fact that he earns his living fighting with his gloved fists in the prize ring, he is a humble man of powerful religious convictions.

The scrupulously observed ritual of blessing himself before and after each bout is no show-off stunt; Carmen simply wouldn't feel right if he didn't do it, and he doesn't care what anybody thinks about it. "I know some of them think I'm laying it on," he says quietly, "but that doesn't bother me. I'd be bothered only if people thought I was trying to get in good with God just to win the fight. That's not the idea at all. I bless myself before the fight to ask God to keep me from getting badly hurt, and after the fight I do it to thank God for taking care of me. It wouldn't be right to ask Him to help me win; He's got more important things to worry about."

It's just like Carmen to worry about being a nuisance. As you get to know him, you find it hard to believe that a man who is such a tiger in the ring, asking no quarter and giving none, can be such a gentle person outside of it. But that's the way it is with Carmen Basilio.

He probably learned his lessons in getting along with other people when he was growing up on the Basilio onion farm at Canastota, New York. He was the seventh of ten children, and in a family as large as that, everybody has to consider the feelings of the others. Everybody has to work, too, and Carmen did his share. Onion farmers in upper New York State grow their crops on what they call "the muck," old land enriched by the fill of decomposed cedar trees. It is black and gooey and dirty, and it is no exaggeration to say that, as much as anything else, the "muck" encouraged Carmen to take up boxing for a living.

Actually, Carmen insists (and his brothers and sisters bear him out), he wanted to be a fighter from the time he was eight years old and used to work out with a pair of kid's gloves from Montgomery Ward on a battered punching bag hanging from a tree in back of the farmhouse. "I always had an idea I'd like it," he says, "and I knew I'd like the money.

My idol was Jimmy Braddock, the old heavy-weight champ. I read all the stories about him—how he came off the docks and the relief rolls to lick Maxie Baer for the heavyweight championship of the world, and made enough money to last him the rest of his life. It made a big impression on me. I wanted to be exactly like Jim. I cried like a baby the night Joe Louis knocked him out."

The first time Carmen put on real boxing gloves and got into a regulation ring was when he was fourteen years old and a high school student in Canastota. In the one year that he went to high school before he left to spend all of his time working on the farm, Carmen took part in only one official match against boxers from a rival school. He won his bout with a technical knockout in the second round. That was during World War II, and Carmen was needed on the farm more than he was in school.

His next opportunity to box came when, at the age of seventeen, he enlisted in the U. S. Marine Corps and was shipped out for two years of overseas duty at Guam and Pearl Harbor. In the last six months of his hitch he filled out an application blank for the All-Navy Boxing Championships and got himself licked in his very first fight. But he wasn't a bit discouraged, and when he was discharged from the Corps in November, 1947, he promptly entered both the AAU and Golden Gloves tournaments in Syracuse, the nearest big city to the family farm. He didn't win any championships but he showed enough ability to encourage him to turn professional.

As a pro, Carmen won his first nine bouts before he was brought back to earth by losing a couple of tough ones in a row. Unluckily for him, he looked his worst whenever his managers, the three Amos brothers, booked him into a Syracuse ring. Maybe he was unnerved by the knowledge that so many of his old friends and neighbors, and relatives too, had come to see him. Whatever it was, Carmen made a habit of putting on a poor fight in his own backyard, and as a result the gates for his bouts were poor and he made very little money.

The low point of his early professional career came in December, 1950, when he lost a decision at Madison Square Garden to a tough journeyman fighter named Vic Cardell. Carmen was leading in the fight when, in the fifth round, Cardell blocked one of his punches with an elbow. The impact broke a bone in Carmen's hand, and he had to stay out of action for a while.

"What a Christmas that was!" Carmen says now with a wry grin. "Kay and I had been married for about a year. On our first date, I took her to a fight. Can you imagine? What a beginning! It took me eleven months to get her to marry me, and then, inside of a year, it looked as though I wasn't going to be able to support her. A fighter who can't fight isn't much use around the house. We were lucky, though. Kay was able to go back to work, and I got a job in a factory that made electrical parts, so we got by. I was making $55 a week, I remember."

To pick up a few extra dollars for Christmas, Carmen, with his broken hand still in a cast, persuaded some of his Syracuse friends to get him a job shoveling snow from the city streets the week before the holiday. He worked three nights, at eight dollars a night, and the $24 he was paid helped make the holiday a little brighter.

Things looked up for Carmen early in 1951, not only because his hand healed but also because the death of one of the Amos brothers

meant that he had to make some other man-
agerial arrangements. Johnny DeJohn and Joe
Netro of Syracuse have managed him from that
day to this. At the same time, an old buddy of
Carmen's, Norman Rothschild, who owned a little restaurant across the street from the Syracuse
Arena, was beginning to promote fights in the
city. He was convinced that Carmen, coming
from the onion-farming country right outside
the city, could be built up into a real home-
town hero. Rothschild got him a match with
Chuck Davey, the educated southpaw from
Michigan State, but Carmen got a tough break
when a split decision in his favor was changed
to a draw because the referee didn't mark his
score card clearly.

What angered Carmen even more was the
failure of the Syracuse newspapers to support
him. The Syracuse *Herald-Journal* called the
original descision in Carmen's favor "a gift
verdict." Its own card, the newspaper said, had
been 7–2–1 in favor of Davey. That outraged
Basilio, but he thought he knew what the trouble was. "Syracuse," Carmen says, "is strictly
a college town. Roy Simmons, the University
boxing coach, was a big Davey fan. The boxing writers in town all listen to him, and he

sold them the idea that Davey was a master boxer and I was a big nothing. Davey, of course, was a college man from Michigan State, a fighter with a degree. I was just a tough kid from the wrong side of the tracks. When the writers watched the fight, they saw only what they had expected to see, what they wanted to see. When I made a good move, or landed a good punch, they didn't quite believe it because they didn't really see it. They only saw what Davey did, because that was what they had come to see."

Carmen thought he had been robbed, but he refused to be discouraged. For one thing, he had earned a substantial pay check from the surprisingly large $25,000 gate, and, for another, he was sure he would be able to beat Davey in a return bout. The rematch was held in Chicago, Davey's home town, and Carmen never had a chance. He was firmly established as a major-league boxer, though, and that was something.

Carmen never has been one to do things the easy way. He got another Chicago match, this time with Billy Graham, a smooth stylist from New York, and Graham gave him an artistic shellacking in full view of a national television

audience. The stock of the little man from
Canastota sank like a stone in water. Even some
of his greatest admirers in the press box began
to think that he was simply a game little fighter
who lacked the boxing ability and the punching
power to hold his own against opponents of
true class.

But Norm Rothschild, who was still busy
promoting fights in Syracuse, didn't see it that
way at all. He thought Carmen had a world
of ability and merely had been the victim of
some bad breaks. He matched him with Sammy
Giuliani, and Carmen knocked Sammy out in
three rounds. He matched him with Carmen
Fiore, and Basilio knocked Fiore out in nine
rounds. Then, with the support and cooperation
of the International Boxing Club, Rothschild
put Carmen in with Billy Graham for the
welterweight championship of New York State,
a title that nobody had even thought of for a
long time but that seemed useful as an advertising build-up for the occasion.

Graham was one of the IBC's big drawing
cards. Most boxing insiders thought he would
make short work of Carmen. But Basilio didn't
climb through the ropes that night to take a
beating. "I knew it was going to be a tough

fight," he says. "Billy was the smartest fighter I'd ever faced. He knew how to keep you off balance, and he had a concrete chin. But I was sure I could get him if I remembered what I had learned in the first fight and didn't try to get cute with him. In this business, you know, you should never try to box a boxer. You fight him; you try to beat him around the body."

That's exactly what Carmen did, and the tactics won the fight for him. He pounded Graham hard through the twelve rounds they fought, and he won the decision handily. He was the welterweight champion of New York State, a title that wouldn't have been of any importance if it hadn't been for the fact that the New York Commission took it seriously and used it as a weapon to bludgeon Kid Gavilan, the world champion, into giving Basilio a shot at the title. It was good politics for the New York officials to force Gavilan to meet Carmen; there were a lot of voters in the upper part of the state who wanted their local boy to have a chance at the championship. There were some boxing fans who thought Carmen wasn't ready for Gavilan yet, but the way it turned out, he almost stole the title.

It all went back to the spring of 1953 when Gavilan visited Syracuse for an over-the-weight, non-title fight with Danny Womber. Given no chance at all against the skillful, battle-toughened champion, Womber crowded Gavilan all night and took a close decision away from him. Carmen sat at ringside and watched every move with the intense interest of the professional. At one point he said to Norm Rothschild, "Did you see what I saw? When Gavilan has to back up, he isn't the same fighter at all. He can be hit. And especially by a left hook. I could give him a lot of trouble."

Carmen gave the Cuban champion so much trouble that he came within one-tenth of a second of stealing the title. He put his theory to work as soon as the fight began, carrying the fight to Gavilan every second, forcing him back on his heels and giving the champion no opportunity to settle into the rhythm of his punching pattern. Again and again he would wave his left hand in front of Gavilan's face, and just as the Kid got set to defend himself against a left hook, Carmen would fire a left uppercut. His stance was that of a righty but he confused Gavilan by repeatedly offering a righthand lead, as a lefthander would be ex-

pected to do. It was easy for Carmen because
he is ambidextrous. In the beginning, he was a
lefty, and he still writes, pitches, and eats left-
handed. But when he became a professional
boxer, he made up his mind that the odds were
stacked against a lefty, and he adopted an or-
thodox stance. He did all right with it, too,
as Gavilan can testify.

In the second round, Carmen started a left
hook, hesitated, changed it to a left uppercut,
and smashed the fist squarely on Gavilan's jaw.
Angered, the Kid charged at Carmen. Basilio,
giving no ground, fought back with a three-
punch combination, a left, a right, and a thun-
derous left hook. The last one in the series was
a bull's-eye to the jaw, and it knocked Gavilan
down. The champion took a nine-count before
he was able to stagger uncertainly to his feet.
But he pulled himself together and went on to
win the decision by the narrowest of margins.

When the reporters crowded into Basilio's
dressing room after the fight and fired their
hundreds of questions at him, about all Carmen
was willing to say was, "It was a good fight.
I'm not going to complain about it. He won
the fight but I'll get all the publicity, watch
and see."

He did, too. Carmen's brave stand had caught the imagination of the fight public, and everybody felt drawn to him. Sympathy couldn't give him the title he had just missed winning, but it could and did serve him well in the future. People liked him and wanted to see him fight. Their affection meant money in the bank to the big promoters and assured Carmen of a fair shake when it came to bookings. His purse from the Gavilan fight alone was enough to buy him and Kay the six-room house in Chittenango in which they still live.

Unhappily, a set of infected tonsils, which he didn't know about until too late, spoiled Carmen's chances of doing well in his first couple of post-Gavilan fights. He was held to a draw by Pierre Langlois in Syracuse and then fought another draw with Italo Scortichini in Miami. Once again his reputation was on the skids. But after the bad tonsils were removed, Carmen bounced right back. He beat Langlois and he beat Scortichini, and he beat everybody else the International Boxing Club put in front of him.

Meanwhile, Kid Gavilan went to Philadelphia and left the title there with Johnny Saxton, a skillful boxer but a light hitter. Basilio and his

managers promptly clamored for a match with
Saxton, but in the mysterious ways of the fight
game, Saxton chose instead to meet Tony De-
Marco in Boston. Johnny got $40,000 for the
fight but it cost him his brand-new championship; DeMarco knocked him out in the four-
teenth round. Once again, Basilio's camp demanded a title match. Much of the political
power of the State of New York got behind
Carmen's crusade. At one point, a New York
State Senator rose in the Legislature at Albany
and demanded that the lawmakers consider
measures to outlaw boxing in the state if Basilio
weren't given a shot at the title. Julius Helfand,
the chairman of the New York Commission,
joined in with a ringing call for a Basilio-DeMarco
fight. The net result of all the shouting was
that, in his sixty-third professional bout, on the
night of June 10, 1955, Carmen got his second
chance to win the welterweight championship of
the world.

It was a hard fight between two determined
little men, the one grimly resolved to hold on
to his prize and the other just as stubbornly
set on wresting it loose. Governor and Mrs.
Averell Harriman of New York were among
the 9,170 excited spectators who crowded into

the Onondaga County War Memorial Auditorium in Syracuse to witness the battle, paying a total of $119,794 for the privilege. They saw a rousing fight. Neither man showed any interest in the refinements of boxing; both preferred to slug it out in the middle of the ring, looking for the big punch that might lead to a knockout. For a good part of the bout, DeMarco, carrying the fight to Basilio in the manner of a true champion, had the home-town hero bewildered as he landed a succession of solid rights and lefts from long range. Basilio, with his short arms, is ineffective when he can't get close to his opponent, and he had his troubles in the first half of the fight.

In the ninth round, Carmen was able to move inside a few wild DeMarco punches and pound home some crushing blows to the body. These shots slowed up the Boston fighter considerably and gave Carmen the chance he had been waiting for. Early in the tenth, Tony tried to rush the challenger, but Carmen boldly wrestled him into position for a series of short but punishing lefts and rights to the head. The last punch of the flurry, a thudding right to the jaw, sent DeMarco crashing to the canvas. He got up at the count of seven, but he was tired and hurt. Instinctively he backtracked, trying to gain time to compose himself. But Basilio charged after him, swinging freely, knowing he was in no danger himself and eager to put an end to it. A two-fisted attack to the head knocked down Tony for the second time, but the game champion wasn't going to give up easily. He got to his feet just as the referee, Harry Kessler, counted eight, and before Carmen could move in to throw another punch, the bell rang and saved DeMarco from further punishment.

In the eleventh round, DeMarco showed the hoarsely shouting crowd what champions are made of. Instead of retreating from the fiercely attacking Basilio's flailing fists, he boldly resumed the role of aggressor and began peppering Carmen's rugged face with stinging punches that lacked knockout power but that clearly gave Basilio the message that he had a lot of fighting to do before he could knock the crown off Tough Tony's head.

Between rounds, Carmen listened carefully to the advice of his managers. So far, they told him, it was a close fight. Carmen was doing fine now, but DeMarco had won all those points in the early rounds, and the champion always got the edge in a close one. Tony was tired, you could see that. The smart thing to do would be to go after him hard and try for a knockout. Basilio nodded soberly, strode out to the middle of the ring, and knocked DeMarco out.

He did it with a mighty barrage of punches that he fired without letup, staggering DeMarco with looping shots to the head and demolishing him utterly with explosive blows to the body that left him without the strength to defend himself. Tony was reeling helplessly, his muscular body sagging, his knees buckling, when referee Kessler sprang between the fighters and led the Boston boy to the safety of his corner. Carmen Basilio, the doughty little warrior from Chittenango, out of Canastota, the idol of Syracuse and of all Central New York, was the winner and the new welterweight champion of the world. He got down on one knee in the center of the ring, while the shouting raged around him, and blessed himself.

Two weeks later, still in the first flush of his glory, Carmen sat in a gleaming new white Cadillac convertible on the main street of the village of Chittenango, grinning happily while his friends, relatives and neighbors threw a parade for him. A pleasant-looking young man wearing horn-rimmed glasses approached the car and leaned in to talk to Carmen. "I'm the Reverend William Cherry," the young man said, "the new Baptist minister."

"Yes, sir," Carmen said, shaking hands firmly. "I'm glad to know you."

"I just wanted to ask you, Carmen," the Reverend Cherry said, "why you knelt down and prayed after you won the fight. You don't often see a boxer do that."

"He helped me," Carmen said simply. "I thanked Him."

"Had you planned ahead of time to do that?" the minister wanted to know.

"No," Carmen told him honestly. "I just felt thankful, that's all."

The minister's face lighted up. "That's fine," he said. "A lot of fighters appeal to the Lord before the fight, but they forget all about Him afterward. Keep up the good work."

The Chittenango Volunteer Fire Brigade Band began loudly to play "From the Halls of Montezuma," in honor of Carmen's thirty-three months of service with the Marine Corps, and the car in which Carmen was riding swung sharply into the line of march and headed down

Genesee Street. Proudly smiling crowds of ordinary people, workmen and their wives and
their children, lined the curbs to pay tribute
to the onion farmer's son who had gone out
into the world and won for himself fame and
fortune of a sort they had never dared dream
of. They looked fondly upon him and they re-
joiced in what he had done.

It hadn't always been that way, as Carmen
well remembers. There was a time when the
people who knew him best, indeed some of his
own flesh and blood who loved him best,
thought so little of his ability that they openly
derided it. Johnny DeJohn, one of his managers, remembers when the boys in the sports
hangouts used to make fun of him for bothering to take over Carmen's contract. "What 'cha
gonna do with him?" they demanded. "You
really gonna let him fight Chuck Davey? That
guy will put him into retirement."

"It's different now," Carmen says. It is different because Carmen was willing to give a
full measure of effort to his occupation. He cut
no corners; he spared himself no sweat or pain.
Irving Robbins, who operates the Main Street
Gymnasium in Syracuse, can testify eloquently
to the way Carmen worked to perfect his skills.

"I've been around boxing for over thirty-five years," Robbins said, "and I've never seen anybody like him. Nobody trains like him, nobody. You know, it's about forty miles round trip from Chittenango or Canastota to the gym here, but when Carmen's in training, nothing can keep him away. I can remember when Johnny DeJohn and Joe Netro were managing Johnny's brother, Joey. Lots of times they'd be here waiting for Joey to come in for a workout, and he'd never show up. He was getting big purses in those days, too. But Carmen, who was fighting for peanuts, like $142 for a fight in Wilkes-Barre, was here every single day. He'd come bouncing in as if there was no place else in the world he'd rather be, and he'd carry his own water bottle and towel, wrap his hands in tape all by himself, and work and work. Even when it snowed, he'd still drive all the way into town for his workout, and a lot of others who lived a couple of blocks away would stay home. I remember once, before a holiday weekend, I wanted to close the place for four days. Carmen balked. He said he couldn't see a four-day layoff at all. Two days was okay, he said, but four days was too much. That's the kind of desire he had."

That kind of desire has paid off for Basilio in jackpot style. It not only made him a champion but enabled him to participate in some of the richest boxing gates of his time. After he won the title from DeMarco, he gave Tony a re-match in Boston and beat him again in a ferociously bruising fight. Once again, DeMarco was in command throughout the first eight rounds. In the seventh, Tony hit Carmen so hard with a long right that Carmen temporarily lost all feeling in his left foot. He was within an ace of going down for the first time since he had graduated from the preliminary ranks. But he held his feet tenaciously, too proud to take a count, and between rounds he shook his numb left foot vigorously until the blood began circulating in it again and feeling flooded back.

He took a beating in the eighth as DeMarco went all out for a knockout, but he gave no ground at all, and Tony proved to be his own worst enemy as he wore himself out punching away at Basilio's granite chin and magnificently trained body. From the ninth on, DeMarco had nothing left; it was Basilio's fight to win, and Carmen knew it. He mounted a furious assault that swiftly wore down the ex-champion, and he finished it with a knockout flourish at

1:54 of the twelfth round. It had taken him exactly two seconds longer than had the first fight.

After those two brawls with Basilio, Tony DeMarco was finished as a top-flight boxer; he never again was able to muster the strength, speed and skill that had enabled him at least for a while to stand at the top of his profession. Carmen, on the other hand, went on to bigger and better things, although he didn't always win. Win or lose, he was a gilt-edged drawing card, the people's favorite fighter, and his strong hands and stout heart earned him a fortune.

He lost the welterweight title to Johnny Saxton at Chicago in March, 1956, on a decision that the New York *Herald-Tribune* said was "so rank that the boos of the crowd are still echoing through Chicago Stadium." He won it back in a furious fight at Syracuse six months later, knocking his man out in the ninth round. Saxton's handlers had conceived the notion that Carmen couldn't win if he were kept moving backward, and Johnny obediently moved in on him and tried to force him to backpedal. It was curious strategy for a boxer who is essentially a counterpuncher, and Carmen feasted upon it. He just stood there, flat-footed, and destroyed the lithe Saxton with some of the most punishing body blows anyone at the ringside ever had seen. Later, the two men met for a third time, at Cleveland, but it was no contest at all. Carmen took Saxton out in two rounds. As one reporter said, "It was just bang, bang, and into the shower."

After he had finished with Saxton, Basilio's fortunes became entangled with those of Sugar Ray Robinson. Robinson had won back his middleweight championship from Gene Fullmer and was looking for a big-money match. His opponent would have to be someone the public would accept as worthy of him but at the same time not too big or too devastatingly powerful to make the match dangerous for a 36-year-old fighter. Basilio looked like a gold mine to Sugar Ray, and negotiations were opened promptly for a rare duel between two popular and respected champions.

Carmen had no special desire to move up to the middleweight class but he was keenly aware that he could make more money out of one match with Robinson than he could make in two years of fighting ordinary opponents. Before the crowd began to gather at Yankee Stadium in New York on the night of September 23, 1957, for what was being billed by the sportswriters as one of the great fights of the century, Carmen had been guaranteed the whopping sum of $110,000 by the theater television people who were expecting their closed-circuit screenings in movie houses to produce a million-dollar gate. Robinson, acknowledged to be the big draw, was being guaranteed an incredible $255,000.

Carmen listened courteously when some of his old friends tried to convince him that he was taking too much of a risk going in against a man who would outweigh him by eight or nine pounds and have the advantage of four and a half inches in height. Carmen, the skillful veteran of 147 fights (143 wins and 4 losses) listened but didn't agree. For one thing, he thought the pay was worth the risk, and for another, he was convinced that he had a good chance to win. He knew he could take a good punch if he had to, and he knew he was seven years younger than Robinson. He intended to keep the pressure on Sugar Ray every minute and make those years count.

That's exactly what Carmen did. He carried the fight to the Harlem boxing master all the way, hooking to the body and the head, digging his strong right under the heart and crossing it to Robinson's jaw. He was in trouble only in the twelfth round, when Sugar Ray gave a vivid demonstration of his days of glory by crashing a wickedly hard right to Carmen's jaw and following it up with a smashing left and then another right to the jaw. They were knockout punches, and they would have finished almost any other man in the ring today. But Basilio shook them off; he was hurt, but he refused to yield. He held on, and he lasted out the storm and went on to win by a 2–1 decision of the officials, a decision that he had earned richly.

He wasn't so lucky in their return bout, staged in Chicago Stadium on the night of March 25, 1958. Carmen had had a frantically busy winter. He was the number one attraction on the banquet circuit, the recipient of more trophies and plaques and scrolls than any other professional athlete in the country. He was the general favorite to win the fight. And he might well have won it, too, except that he found himself up against not only a grimly resolute and still great Sugar Ray, but also a massive dose of bad luck.

In the fifth round, one of Robinson's punches completely closed Basilio's left eye, which had begun to suffer damage as early as the third round. For the rest of the bitter fight, Carmen was a one-eyed man, and, as such, no match for a sharpshooting puncher like Robinson. He lost the decision, another split 2–1 affair. In losing, however, he not only deposited another huge sum of money in the bank—almost $300,000— but he also added luster to his reputation as a brave and accomplished fighter. He never backed away from his tormentor, and when the last bell rang, Robinson was every bit as weary and hurt as the loser. Carmen had hit him so hard and so often in the body that Sugar Ray was moved to say, "Even the soles of my feet hurt."

The boxing writers said it was one of the great fights of all time. They wrote, respectfully, that these two great champions had given the millions who saw the fight at the stadium and in the theaters a rare display of gallantry and courage. "Men like Robinson and Basilio," said one writer, "do not fight just for a purse. There is honor and bravery in it, too."

Carmen Basilio may or may not have other great nights in the ring, but no matter how long he continues his career, or how many victories he achieves, he already has done what most men spend a lifetime doing. The name of Carmen Basilio has been given a meaning that will last long after the lifetime of the humble, courageous, plain man who has worn it so proudly.

Chapter Three

ALEX OLMEDO, THE TENNIS PLAYER
WHO LIKES EVERYBODY

Salvatore Olmedo, the hard-working caretaker of the tennis club in Arequipa, Peru, cares about nothing in the world except his family, his faith and the game of tennis. He not only does the work of caring for the courts at Arequipa, he also serves as the club professional. It means hard work, long hours, and not very much money, but Salvatore likes it and it has been enough for him to take care of his wife and their six children. He never has asked for anything more.

If, indeed, he ever dreamed of anything more, his wildest flight of imagination could not possibly have conjured up the picture of one of his most cherished pupils—his second son, Alejandro—winning the Davis Cup single-handed and becoming the champion amateur tennis player of the whole world. If someone had told him that such a thing might conceivably happen, he probably would have just shaken his head and walked away. He knew that little Alex was a good tennis player, that he had a graceful and sure way of hitting the ball, but there are a great many good tennis players in all the countries of the world. It did not occur to Salvatore that his boy had the ability to walk in the footsteps of champions like Don Budge, Jack Kramer, Pancho Gonzales and Lew Hoad.

Young Alex, part Spanish, part Inca, and all boy, brought his tennis talents forcibly to his father's attention for the first time when he was fourteen years old, a student at St. Thomas Aquinas School in Lima. Without bothering to ask permission, he took a tennis racket out of a rack in Salvatore's pro shop and entered a local men's singles tournament. The punishment decreed for his misdeed probably would have been more severe if Alex hadn't had the good judgment to win the tournament. It was an amazing accomplishment for so young a boy, playing against grown men, and no matter how hard he tried to be stern about it, Salvatore Olmedo couldn't help but be proud of his son.

That was the beginning. Allowed to keep the racket on condition that he work off its cost by doing a full schedule of jobs around the tennis courts, Alex began to take regular lessons from his father. By the time he was fifteen, he won the South Peruvian men's championship and added three successive national junior championships to his collection. Just about this time, an American professional named Stan Singer, a former U.C.L.A. player, came to Peru at the invitation of coffee millionaire Jorge Harten to develop a junior tennis program in the country. Naturally, Singer's attention centered upon Olmedo. "He doesn't even hold his racket properly," he told his sponsor, Harten, "but this kid has a world of ability. He can go places if he ever gets a chance."

The chance came for Alex when, at Singer's urging, a group of Peruvian businessmen made up a fund to send him to the United States. It was a stab in the dark because no one, including Singer, knew exactly what the boy would be able to do when he got to the States; he had failed in several attempts to win a college scholarship, largely because he didn't know how to speak English. But the risk appealed to Alex's sense of adventure, and he leaped at the opportunity. It was decided that he would go to Los Angeles, in the heart of the U.S.A.'s tennis belt, and a ticket was bought for him on a banana boat that was sailing to Miami.

With about two hundred dollars in his pocket, and a couple of his father's tennis rackets carefully packed away in his luggage, Alex set out to conquer the world. But, as he is honest enough to tell you, it never once occurred to him, not even when he was saying his prayers and asking the blessing of Mamacita, the Blessed Mother, on his journey, that that was exactly what he was going to do.

One thing in Alex's favor was that he didn't expect anything to be handed to him on a silver platter. He was willing to work for whatever he might be able to get. On the boat, for example, he helped out as a cabin boy during the slow, three-week journey. He knew he was going to need every dollar of his modest bankroll when he got to the United States. He had heard how much things cost there. When the boat finally docked at Miami, he showed his thrifty nature again by passing up the more comfortable transcontinental trains for a long ride to Los Angeles in an economical bus. "It wasn't bad," he says now. "My biggest trouble was that all I knew how to say in English was 'Yes,' 'No,' and 'Coke, please.'"

When he arrived in Los Angeles, Alex had only a little more than a hundred dollars in his wallet, and he knew the name of only one man in the city. This was Joe Cianci, one of Stan Singer's old friends. Cianci, who ran the Poinsettia Park Tennis Club courts, a public setup, didn't turn away the strange boy from Peru. He gave him a job in the pro shop, doing the same kind of work Alex had done for his father back home. Even more important than the job, which earned Alex enough money to pay for his room and board, and the tennis lessons he gave him, Cianci saw to it that Olmedo enrolled in night school and learned English. Then, when the time was right, he introduced him to people who were able to get him a scholarship to Modesto Junior College. Now Alex's American adventure began to move into high gear.

A young tennis player who shows the kind

of promise that Alex Olmedo showed does not lack for assistance, if the tennis officials make up their minds that he is serious about the game and will make the most of his opportunities. At Modesto, Alex played on the same team with Mike Green and Gerry Moss, two of the most highly regarded junior prospects. He acquitted himself well in competition with them. He gained still more attention when he won the national public parks junior singles championship, and helped win the doubles and mixed doubles titles, too. On the strength of these victories, he crossed over to the other side of the tracks, in a manner of speaking, and found himself a member in good standing of the country club set, welcome even in the exclusive Los Angeles Tennis Club, where the kingpins of the game play each other day in and day out, sharpening their weapons on the kind of opposition only another champion can provide.

Things were looking up for Alex. His English had improved to the point where he was no longer always in danger of being picked up by the police as a Mexican "wetback," an illegal immigrant, and his tennis was becoming interesting enough to catch the eye of the game's No. 1 man in Southern California, Perry T. Jones. Mr. Jones, as he is most respectfully called by his innumerable tennis protégés, thought he saw something in Alex. He saw to it that the cheerful, energetic youngster was given a scholarship to the University of Southern California. There Alex came under the guidance of a sound coach, George Toley, and nothing better could have happened to him. Toley, who had been a high ranking player himself in his younger days, and who has a gift for teaching and inspiring young players, was able to give a lot of attention to Olmedo because he combined his work at U.S.C. with the job of pro at the Los Angeles Tennis Club. He had the boy under his eye both during school hours and after.

In fact, with his father thousands of miles away in Peru, Alex came to look upon Toley as more of a parent than a coach. Toley advised him in his personal life as much as in his tennis tactics; he arranged practice matches for him with the great players who made the club their hangout; and when the youngster was broke, he loaned him money. Nobody, not even Salvatore Olmedo, took more pleasure in Alex's climb to success than George Toley did.

One of the stars against whom Toley pitted Alex was the incomparable Pancho Gonzales, the professional champion who was acknowledged by everyone in the game to be the greatest of all the active players. Gonzales, himself the possessor of one of the most famous cannonball serves of all time, was vastly impressed by the blistering speed with which Alex belted his service across the net. "That serve will make history some day," Pancho said admiringly. And it soon developed that the big champion knew what he was talking about.

Alex caught the attention of the whole tennis world in the summer of 1956 when he won the national intercollegiate singles championship. This is an important title, not a ham-and-egg trophy by any means, and in winning it Olmedo placed his name on a list that includes some of the most shining stars the game has ever known. He wasn't able to defend the title in 1957 because U.S.C. had been suspended from intercollegiate competition as punishment for violating the football recruiting rules. But in 1958 he won the tournament for the second time, proving convincingly that he was no fluke champion.

By now, there was no question that Alex had

the makings of a major-league tennis star. True, he never had been able to get past the round of sixteen in the national singles championship at Forest Hills, and on his one trip to Wimbledon, in the spring of 1957, he had been bounced out of the tournament in the first round by Australia's Mervyn Rose. But he had all the shots a champion needs. All he had to do, most tennis people felt, was to discipline his shots and his temperament; he had to buckle down to the realization that success in big-time tennis does not come easily, even to a naturally gifted player. It takes sweat and determination and the instinct to fight back gladly after you have been beaten. Alex is a friendly young fellow, happy go lucky, and he hadn't learned yet to be tough.

Convinced that "the Chief," as the other tennis players call Alex because of his part-Indian heritage, had both the ability and the character to handle the assignment, the newly appointed captain of the United States Davis Cup team, Perry Jones, began campaigning early in the summer of 1958 for Alex's appointment to the Cup squad. Not surprisingly, he ran into a storm of opposition. It wasn't that the members of the selection committee, or for that matter the members of the press, didn't like Olmedo, or didn't think he showed great promise as a player; it was simply that they didn't like the idea of naming a foreigner to represent the U.S. in an international competition. Alex was a citizen of Peru and he made it clear that he intended to remain one. The Davis Cup rules provide for the appointment of a foreigner to the team of another country provided the foreigner has lived in his "adopted" country a minimum of five years, and provided the country of his birth does not have a Davis Cup team of its own. Alex, who had been living in the United States since 1954, met both of these requirements. It was perfectly legal for him to be named to a place on the U.S. team. But Jim Moffett, the chairman of the Cup committee, was hesitant. He feared that a storm of criticism would result. Doughty old Perry Jones, whose responsibility it was to take the team to Australia and try to win back the cup, argued fiercely. His case was strengthened when Alex teamed with Hamilton Richardson to win the national doubles championship at Brookline, Massachusetts. It became harder and harder to overlook the Chief.

Olmedo himself, eager to be friends with

everyone, said little as the controversy raged. About all he would tell the newspapermen, aside from the fact that he didn't want to give up his Peruvian citizenship, was that, "If I am selected, I will consider it a great honor. I would like very much to play in the Davis Cup."

In the end, against the better judgment of Mr. Moffett and quite a few other influential tennis officials, Alex made it. He was appointed to the team, and, along with Barry MacKay and Ham Richardson, he stunned the Australians by pinning a 3–2 defeat on them in the Challenge Round matches in Brisbane.

As is always the case in such an operation, it was a team triumph. It was Perry Jones's triumph, for he had put Alex on the team. It was Jack Kramer's triumph, for the master professional had devoted two months of his time to training the American team for the effort. Certainly it was Ham Richardson's triumph, for he had helped at a crucial moment. But, most of all, essentially, it was Alejandro Olmedo's triumph. For Alex came pretty close to winning the historic trophy all by himself.

Alex drove the first nail into the coffin of Australia's hopes by taking the measure of Mal

Anderson, Australia's No. 2 player, in four rugged sets, 8–6, 2–6, 9–7, 8–6. The weather was hot and steamy, and Alex obviously was calling upon every ounce of his strength, but he pulled through, and the United States team was very much in business with a 1–0 lead. The Australians tied it at 1–1 when Ashley Cooper defeated MacKay. But in the third match, the doubles, Richardson and Olmedo teamed to wallop Anderson and Neale Fraser, 10–12, 3–6, 16–14, 6–3, 7–5, in a dramatic marathon match that ranks with the most exciting duels in the history of the Cup competition. Hardly anyone in the great crowd of 18,500 people in the Milton Tennis Stadium gave the U.S. players a chance after they had lost the first two sets. But when they pulled out the third set, 16–14, with Olmedo serving like a wizard, the tide of battle changed. You could see the confidence growing in every shot Alex and Ham made. They were grimly determined to win, and win they did.

Barry MacKay still couldn't quite make it as he lost to Mal Anderson in the third singles match, but it didn't matter because the colorful Chief had done it again. Alex had already locked up the Cup victory with a smashing

6–3, 4–6, 6–4, 8–6 defeat of Cooper to put a proper finishing touch on the most wonderful week of his twenty-two years.

"I feel great," Alex told the reporters who crowded around him after the decisive match. "I feel happy. I feel fabulous."

He had every reason to feel that way. Back home in Arequipa, his father was smiling dazedly as the news came in that his boy had climbed to the very top of the tennis world. In the United States, people were speculating that Alex was a sure shot to become the new Don Budge, the new Jack Kramer. A rich professional contract loomed on his horizon. Things were a whole lot different for Alex than they had been when he got off that banana boat at Miami and thriftily bought himself a ticket on a cross-country bus to Los Angeles. He was sitting on top of the world.

His perch was even more secure after the Australian National Championships were played in January. For in that one, Alex fought his way through the draw to meet Neale Fraser in the final round, and won, 6–1, 6–2, 3–6, 6–3, to take the title away from the shores of Australia for the first time in eight years. It looked very much as though Alex had matured completely as a tennis player. He covered court like a cat, and his shots rang with power. His service was harder than ever, and more accurate. He made old pro Jack Kramer smile, partly out of pride that Alex was making him look so good as a teacher, and partly in anticipation of the great matches that could be put together when Alex turned pro and tangled with such players as Pancho Gonzales, Lew Hoad and the rest of Kramer's touring troupe.

Any doubts that some people had about Alex's ability to play as well indoors as he had outdoors vanished after his exciting showing in the 57th annual National Indoor Championships at the 7th Regiment Armory in New York. The most conservative of the tennis writers felt that Olmedo had little chance to win the tournament, his first on boards. They hoped merely that he would play well and make new friends in the big city. But he fooled them all by battling to the final round and there, in a genuinely memorable match, upsetting the defending champion, Dick Savitt, an old hand at indoor play, by the marathon scores of 7–9, 6–3, 6–4, 5–7, 12–10. At the end, the 3,500 spectators were every bit as exhausted as the players were; it had been a great match, and the fun-loving Chief from Peru had proved once again that he is a dangerous foe in a hard fight, and that, although he liked everybody to be his friend, he also likes to win.

Then, finally, Alex was able to go back to California, back to school, and back to a slightly quieter life for a while. He was able, after the tense months of competition, to indulge himself once again in his passion for Wild West movies. He was able to make himself comfortable in his little two-room apartment in Los Angeles, not far from the U.S.C. campus, and amuse himself experimenting with meals cooked entirely out of cans. He was able to take time to write a few longer letters home and tell his father how it had felt to play for the Davis Cup, and, best of all, how it had felt to win.

He was able to thank Mamacita, the Blessed Mother, to whom he had directed all his prayers in those uncertain, homesick, sometimes bitterly discouraging early days in the United States, for all she had done for him. It was quite a lot.

Chapter Four

JUAN MANUEL FANGIO, THE CAREFUL DAREDEVIL

Most people think of racing car drivers as wild men obsessed with the idea of speed. One can hardly blame them; many drivers think of themselves that way. The dashing Marquis de Portago, who was killed during the *Mille Miglia* in Italy early in 1957, once said, "There are only three true sports, mountain climbing, bull fighting, and automobile racing. All the others are mere recreations." What de Portago meant was that the very word "sport" implies taking the sporting risk of losing your life.

But not all successful racing car drivers feel that way. To at least one of them, driving a high-powered, finely-tuned Mercedes-Benz or Maserati is a business to be pursued as cautiously as piloting a Boeing 707 or steering a giant ocean liner or hammering rivets into steel girders on the 39th floor of a new skyscraper. If he were a lesser driver, a nobody in the sport, this man's opinions might not count for anything, but he is the king of all the drivers, the champion of champions, and there is nobody who will not listen earnestly to what Juan Manuel Fangio has to say about automobile racing.

What he has to say is that it is reckless not to place your safety, and the safety of your competitors, ahead of mere victory. It is, he thinks, foolhardy not to take every possible precaution, even if by doing so you reduce your chances of winning. That's why they call Fangio "the careful daredevil." Actually, it isn't correct to call him a "daredevil" at all, except for the undeniable fact that he earns his living in a most hazardous profession. The plain fact is that he takes no chances he doesn't have to take. Marshall Smith, the sports editor of *Life,* said this about him early in 1958:

"Of the millions of motorists in the world, the one most deserving of canonization by the National Safety Council is a phlegmatic, 46-year-old Argentine named Juan Fangio. In this age of high horsepower, super highways and jet getaway, Fangio drives with restraint and unflagging vigilance. He is neither a road hog nor a lane hopper. He never passes on hills or curves. At stop signs he does not merely shift into second; he comes to a dead stop. At all times his eyes are fixed on the road ahead. He does not glance aside to read Burma-Shave signs. He does not even talk to people who are riding in the same car with him since this might cause his attention to wander. In fact, the only thing that distinguishes Juan Fangio from the little old lady who drives along back roads at ten miles per hour is that he is the world's supreme driver of racing automobiles."

It is true that Fangio has a horror of taking unnecessary risks in an automobile. That goes for a regular passenger car as well as a racing car. He is genuinely shocked by the carelessness of the average motorist. "They talk, they look right and left, they enjoy the scenery," he says. "It is no longer a pleasure to be a driver. It is a sacrifice." When he is being driven by someone else, Fangio is as nervous as a cat. He watches the road ahead for traffic lights and for possible obstructions. He stays alert for cars or trucks coming in from side roads, and he is constantly peering ahead to watch out for train crossings. If he is driving himself, he prefers to take the road after midnight when traffic is light. He thinks American drivers are probably the world's best, but he wouldn't dream of riding in a private car in the congested streets of New York City. He prefers taxicab drivers. "They are specialists at their kind of driving," he says with the respect of the true professional. "I would rather have them perform."

But Fangio probably never would have developed such an acute sense of caution if he hadn't been so different in his youth. Then, when he was new at the game of race driving, he was every inch the daredevil driver so many of his fans still imagine him to be. Nothing mattered, in those days, except winning the race. If he hadn't been fortunate, as well as instinctively skillful, Juan never would have lived to be known as the grand old man of the sport. Certainly he never would have become the world champion because he didn't achieve any measure of international fame at all until he was thirty-eight years old, and he had pressed his luck to the fullest for almost twenty years before that.

The son of an Italian plasterer who had migrated to Argentina in search of a better life, Juan Manuel Fangio grew up in a country that was wild about automobile racing. He was born on June 24, 1911, in the vicinity of Balcarce, a pretty town situated in the valley of Argentina's Table Mountains. Because he was born on San Juan's day, it seemed logical to his father to name him Juan. He was the fourth of six children, and because of the large size of the family and the small amount of his father's income as a potato farmer, Juan had to add to the family funds as soon as he was old enough to work. He developed an interest in automobiles when he was nine or ten years old, and as soon as he reached his early teens he was able to earn a little money working as a grease monkey at a local garage. Automobiles soon became his chief interest in life.

At the age of eighteen, Juan was stricken with pneumonia and almost died. Only the most urgent efforts of his doctors and his

mother, and his mother's fervent prayers to Our
Lady, saved his life. His health recovered, Juan
went into the army and served for a year at
the cadet school, Campo de Mayo, outside of
Buenos Aires. There, for the greater part of
his term of service, he was given the assignment of chauffeuring the commanding officer.

Home again in Balcarce, Juan began to think
seriously about the kind of work he wanted to
do. The more he thought about it, the more
he knew that he wanted to be a racing driver.
Automobiles were his great love; his grease
monkey job and his work with cars in the
army had convinced him that nothing else ever
would mean as much to him. So he began to
look for a job as a driver.

Juan could not have thought of a job harder
to get. Balcarce is a small town and a poor one,
and few men there can afford the expense of
racing automobiles. Of course, Balcarce, like
almost every town in the province of Buenos
Aires, had its plain dirt track, and every year
there were a certain number of automobile
races held there. Juan was known around town
as a young man who had worked with automobiles, and because of his experience he often
got the job of assistant driver on racing cars

because the driver knew he could depend upon Juan to fill the role of mechanic in case of trouble.

It wasn't until he was twenty-three years old that Juan drove his first race at the wheel of his own car. It was a race which he never finished because the car, a rebuilt taxicab, virtually fell apart halfway around the course. But not even that dismal experience was enough to discourage Fangio. The more he tried automobile racing, the more he loved it. Before another year was out, he had built a "Model T Ford Special" of his own, using a multitude of spare parts from all kinds of cars to create the finished product. It didn't matter to him that the rear axle was from a Buick, the transmission from a Chevrolet, and the engine block from a Ford; all he cared about was that the car ran easily and powerfully and that it offered him a chance to win the race. The fact that he didn't win a race for a long time didn't discourage him from doing his best; neither was he discouraged by the frequent indications that he had let himself in for a dangerous business. It was the only job he wanted.

It was during the *Tres Arroyos* race in Argentina in 1938 that the danger of racing was made clear to Juan Fangio, the man who was to become the most successful racing driver of his time and also the most skillful and most careful. Juan had got off to a slow start, but he refused to give up. He ate the dust of almost every other car in the race, and his goggles were covered by a thick layer of dirt by the time he had covered his fifth lap. His foot had been pressed to the floor all the way; he knew what an uphill fight he faced. No wonder he was astonished when, at the end of lap No. 5, he was flagged in by the officials.

"What's the matter?" Fangio demanded unhappily as he pulled into the pit.

"Don't you know?" they asked incredulously. "Five drivers have been killed already."

Fangio didn't know, but, as time went on, he became used to the idea. He didn't like it, but he accepted the fact that accidents and injuries, and even sudden deaths, were part of the game. Finally, in 1940, at the age of twenty-nine, Juan won his first race. It was the Gran Premio International del Norte, a brutal 5,932-mile haul from Buenos Aires to Lima and back. Overnight, he was famous—at least, in South America. And overnight, his life changed. He was able to go back to Balcarce and set up a General Motors dealership. He was more than a successful racing driver, he was also a successful businessman. Even his mother, who had bitterly opposed his driving, felt that he had made his mark in the world and that it was a good one.

Juan might have gone on to build an international reputation, and much wealth for himself, within a very few years. Unfortunately for him, and for everyone else, the world was brewing another great war. From 1940 until 1942, he reigned supreme in Argentine road-racing, but then the war kept him out of action until 1947. He worked at his dealership in Balcarce and did what he could to keep the town's automobiles running through the years of the great war.

Juan did not give up his interest in racing; at every opportunity he worked to perfect his skills, reminding himself over and over again, "I must not vegetate." His work as an automobile dealer and a mechanic helped him to keep his hand in and to remind him that when the war was over there would be a need for men like him to revive auto racing. When the need for money pressed him hard, he took a job as a taxicab driver. Between one thing and another, he managed to keep himself going until automobile racing picked up again in 1947. Dictator Juan Perón had come to power in Argentina then, and one of his whims was to make Buenos Aires one of the great automobile racing capitals. The most famous drivers in the world were invited there to race, and Fangio learned much from them.

He also learned much from their cars. His eyes popped out at the sight of the gleaming beauties that the European driving champions brought with them. The Maseratis, Alfa Romeos and Ferraris that he saw in the postwar races taught him how great a difference there was between truly fine equipment and the heavy, unresponsive cars he was used to driving. One of his last lessons in this regard was a frightening accident he had during the Buenos Aires-to-Caracas race in 1948. Speeding through the mountains of Peru late at night, he went off the road and tumbled down the mountainside, pieces of his car flying about his ears. His partner was killed, and for a long time Fangio insisted that he would never race again. But when the Argentinian Automobile Club, created by Perón, offered to provide him with a magnificent new Maserati to drive in the City of Buenos Aires Grand Prix, he couldn't resist. He accepted the automobile, drove it with great success, and was unable to say no when he was asked to join an Argentine team being sent to Europe for the racing program of 1949.

Juan was thirty-eight years old that summer, and the days of his recklessness were over. He drove carefully, with the skill and the wisdom of an old professional, and with a feel for the automobile that came from his years of experience as a mechanic and a dealer as well as a driver. He won the races at Marseilles and at Monza, at San Remo and at Pau and at Perpignan. He entered, in all, ten races, and he won six of them. Back in Argentina, every fresh report of his exploits made him more of a national hero. When he finally returned home, he was given a reception worthy of a conquering general. His reputation at home was secure for all time.

Since then, Fangio has won them all. The roll call of his victories sounds like the blare of trumpets: the Grand Prix of Monaco . . . the Grand Prix of Portugal . . . the Grand Prix of France . . . the Grand Prix of Germany . . . the Grand Prix of Pescara . . . the Grand Prix of Italy . . . the Grand Prix of Argentina . . . and the Grand Prix of Europe, which he won in August of 1954, watched by more than 200,000 wildly excited people who lined the tricky 311-mile course to watch a grimly contested race in which twenty cars started and only ten finished.

Fangio has survived his long years of risking his life in automobile races by following a careful plan of preparation for each event. He finds out everything he can about the course he is going to drive over, and he keeps himself in magnificent physical condition. "I learned years ago," he says, "that an automobile race driver must be in top condition. A man can't play until the early hours of the morning and expect to have sharp reflexes. I watch my diet. I go to bed no later than ten o'clock in the evening during the whole week before the race."

And as race day nears, Juan spends hours every day going over the race course minutely. He studies each turn, bump and weakness in the roadbed. He has been known to walk over a course three or four times in order to be sure of his facts before getting behind the wheel for the race.

"He knows just how much a car can take," one of his rival drivers says, "and he never drives it beyond its capacity. He will run fourth, third and second for mile after mile, never disturbed by the great bursts of speed put on by his younger rivals. He knows all the cars in the race and their potentialities. So he knows when the rival cars are being driven too hard, and he waits. Sooner or later they will come back to him or drop out altogether."

Juan's carefulness never should be confused with reluctance to take the chances that are necessary in his business. Like everyone else, he was appalled by the holocaust at Le Mans, France, in June, 1955, when eighty-seven people were killed in the most shocking disaster ever to overtake the sport of motor racing. Fangio was trailing Mike Hawthorn, the young Englishman, by only a few seconds on the thirty-second lap of the race when Hawthorn headed for his pit. Suddenly veering away from the pit row, Hawthorn caused two drivers whom he had just lapped, Lance Macklin and Pierre Levegh, to crack up. Macklin's car never left the track, but Levegh's Mercedes struck the five-foot bulwark, vaulted it end over end, and rolled over three times. The engine, ripped free of its mountings, shot into space like a shell from a naval gun, and mowed a lethal path through the dense crowd.

It was a horrible, nerve-wracking accident, and no one felt it more keenly than Fangio, who was astoundingly lucky to have been able to weave his way through the wrecks that suddenly dotted the track in front of him. "What luck," he stammered afterward, "I was lucky. I was going to pass Levegh, but he signaled me to stop. Why was I so lucky?"

And yet, shaken though he was, only eight days later Fangio won his third Grand Prix of the year by driving his Mercedes home first in the Dutch Grand Prix at Zandvoort-on-Sea in the Netherlands. Winning the race, the first major racing event since Le Mans, assured Fangio of retaining his world driving championship.

It would be almost impossible these days to find anyone knowledgeable on the subject of automobile racing who would criticize Fangio. Five times the winner of the world driving championship, Juan is the acknowledged master of the trade. Even though he has gone into semi-retirement, and has been succeeded by other champions, Fangio remains the image of the champion in the eyes of most enthusiasts.

Of course, some of his most talented competitors, Eugenio Castellotti, Luigi Musso, Mike Hawthorn and Marquis Alfonso de Portago, are dead—killed in race crashes. But there are plenty of top-flight drivers still in action, and they have yet to take away the mantle that Fangio has worn for so long.

Fangio's position at the top of the heap was never more graphically illustrated than during the week of the Gran Premio de Cuba in Havana in the winter of 1958. Fidel Castro's rebel forces, doing their best to harass the troops and the programs of President Fulgencio Batista, kidnapped Fangio on the eve of the big race. Juan was standing in the lobby of the Lincoln Hotel in Havana, talking to friends, when two armed and disguised rebels stalked into the room. One stood guard at the front door while the other approached Fangio and forced him, at gunpoint, to leave with them. He was driven away in a big, speedy car, and was seen no more until midnight of the day of the race.

The rebels broadcast to the world their hope that the kidnapping of Fangio would embarrass the Batista government. They made it clear that they had no intention of harming the great driver, but even so, Fangio could not have felt especially comfortable in captivity. The most hospitable of kidnappers can become sullen and vengeful if things do not go well.

Fortunately for Fangio, things went very well from the kidnappers' point of view. Not only did the abduction of the star driver create a world-wide sensation, but a tragic crash killed six spectators and injured thirty-one more, and caused the race to be ended far short of the original plan.

Juan was held prisoner for twenty-six hours. "I was transferred three times to three different houses," he said, "and they used three different automobiles. The houses were well furnished residences, and in one of them I saw part of a film of the Gran Premio on television." Finally, after the race was long over, he was driven to a house on the outskirts of Havana and was told to go inside and wait there until someone called for him. The someone turned out to be Rear Admiral Raul Lynch, Argentina's ambassador to Cuba, who had been notified by a rebel spokesman that Fangio awaited him there.

It was a fantastic incident that pointed up, in a comic-opera way, the singular importance of Juan Manuel Fangio's position in the sport of auto racing. It was, as more than one American newspaper pointed out, like kidnapping Mickey Mantle the night before the first game of the World Series.

The year 1958 held still another sensational incident for the old man of the Pampas. For the first time in his proud career, he agreed to drive in the premier automobile race in the United States, the Indianapolis "500." With great advance publicity, Fangio was lured to Indianapolis early in May by the Dayton Steel Foundry Company, which had a special racing car that the heads of the company wanted him to drive. There is no doubt that Juan was offered large sums of money to handle the assignment, but neither is there any question that he was inspired, as he said, by a boyhood longing to drive in this most famous of all American automobile races.

He may also have been inspired by the sarcastic challenges flung at him by Floyd Clymer, a California motor racing magazine publisher who argued bitterly that Fangio could be considered nothing more than a "phony" champion so long as he refused to drive at Indianapolis. Clymer insisted that the speeds Fangio had to maintain to win the Grand Prix road races in Europe and South America were child's play compared with the speeds required to stay in the running at Indianapolis. He missed no opportunity to condemn Fangio as a "phony" who would be exposed quickly if he dared risk his reputation against the kings of the red-brick roadbed at Indianapolis.

When Fangio made it known that he was planning to race in the "500," he was asked bluntly if he was out to shove Clymer's words down his throat. "No," he said through an interpreter—he speaks only a few words of broken English—"I wanted to come because it's one of my life's ambitions."

The traditional three stripes of a rookie Indianapolis driver were painted on the tail of Fangio's car when he showed up for his physical examination, his driving test and his qualifying trials. He passed every test asked of him, and he survived two close brushes with death on the slippery track when speeding cars went into uncontrollable spins right in front of him, but finally he decided to retire from the race before it was time for the qualification trials. "The 500-mile race," he said solemnly to one reporter, "is a dangerous race."

Juan didn't, of course, mean that he was

quitting because he scented too much danger. What he did have in mind was the foolishness of continuing in a race that he simply didn't know enough about. He didn't know the course and he didn't know his car and he didn't know the competing cars. Perhaps most important of all, he didn't think his car was a good one, at least not good enough to win. In short, Juan Fangio was unwilling to risk his reputation under conditions he regarded as unfavorable. And so much had been made of his first assault on the Indianapolis track that he could hardly be blamed for that.

A few months later, Juan announced to the world that he was retiring from all road-racing with the possible exception of a few South American events which he might enter just to keep his hand in. "At a certain age one must make a certain decision," he said to reporters, adding that he expected to devote his time in the future to the automobile industry, "an activity in which I intend to prove useful to my country."

If he sticks to it, he can hardly be blamed for quitting. He has spent the greater part of his life in the cockpits of hurtling automobiles. He has come within a hair's breadth of losing his life at least a dozen times. He has had to keep in strict training. He is tired. Also, he cannot help but wonder if perhaps the law of averages won't soon catch up with him if he continues to drive.

Fangio no longer needs the money that racing brings him. He owns a 2,000-seat movie theater, two service stations, a Chevrolet dealership and a Vespa motor-scooter sales franchise. His name is valuable for advertising endorsements. He earns probably a minimum of $100,000 a year. Juan Perón, the former President and Dictator of Argentina, who gave him his start as a big-time driver and had a claim on him to give his all for the state, is no longer around. Fangio is very much his own man, and he needs neither the money nor the fame that further competition might bring him. His plump, pretty wife, Andreina, who has cleaned his goggles and handed him his coffee through all the years of his racing career, wants him to quit. She is tired of closing her eyes as he roars through another near-miss at 140 miles per hour.

Perhaps in the back of Fangio's mind, as he contemplates a life of well deserved ease, is the persistent, gnawing worry that too few of his rival drivers think as highly as he does of safety on the track. For instance, Juan was the only big-name driver to refuse to compete in the 1957 *Mille Miglia* race in Italy in which Marquis de Portago, his co-driver, and 15 spectators were killed. "No man with a conscience should drive in it," he said sorrowfully, after the sad news had reached him. "All those curves, and all those people . . . and especially, all those children."

The more you talk to Juan Manuel Fangio about the business he has followed most of his life, the more you realize that what he fears most on the course is the reckless, wild young driver who thinks he is tearing around with the boldness of the great Fangio. Actually, Fangio is the most careful driver you could ever hope to meet, even when he is maintaining a speed well in excess of a hundred miles per hour. He knows what he is doing at all times, and he will never risk his neck for a few seconds of time.

The "careful daredevil" wins races because he has only one basic rule, besides common sense. "I don't," he says, "like to see any other driver in front of me."

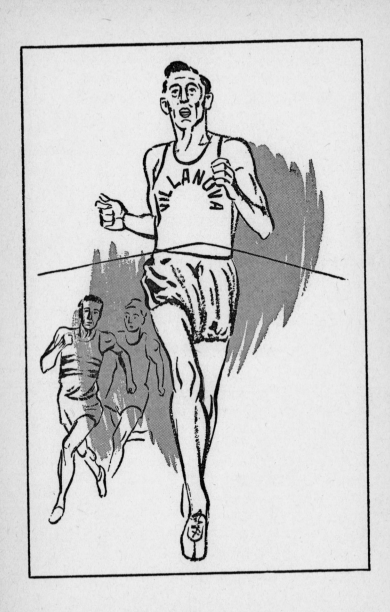

Chapter Five

THE FLYING IRISHMAN, RON DELANY

The small cavalcade of cars winding through the Irish countryside from Limerick to Dublin made a turn in the road and came upon an unexpected sight. The band of De La Salle School, a Christian Brothers institution, was lined up two dozen strong along the roadway with one of the husky young Brothers standing out in front ready to conduct. As soon as he spotted the motorcade, the Brother gave the boys the signal to begin to play. The lead car promptly

slowed, then came to a stop, and out of it
popped a tall, black-haired, angular young man
with the map of Ireland on his face and the
spring of the athlete in his long legs. Grinning,
he ran across the street to thank the boys and
show them the gold medal he had won for Ireland in the Olympic Games far across the
oceans, in Melbourne, Australia.

The boys, with their long tin whistles and
their cymbals and their drums, were wide-eyed
with joy. The most they had expected was a
wave of the hand from this young national
hero as he sped by in his automobile. That he
should take the time to stop his car and stand
here talking with them on the roadside as
though he were just an ordinary human being
like themselves was more than they could bear.
The good Brother, staring at the gold medal
in its velvet box, the first Olympic gold medal
won by an Irishman in thirty-four years, said
emotionally, "You've seen the medal, boys, now
give a cheer all together, hip, hip!" And the
boys cheered wildly as their hero shook hands
with them and turned and ran back to the car.
The Brother followed after him, running awk-
wardly in his cassock, and saying, "You're very

good and kind, Ronnie, very good and kind
indeed!"

In such a way, happily but humbly meeting the
people he had left four years before when he went
to study at Villanova University, near Philadelphia
in the United States, Ronald Michael Delany
of Dublin, Ireland, went home in the winter of
1957. He was twenty-one years old, the greatest
mile runner in the world, the winner of the
Olympic metric mile, the king of the world's
indoor milers, and one of the select group of
runners to have beaten the magic time of four
minutes for the mile. Most of all, he was the
favorite of his countrymen, whose pride in him
and in his accomplishments was great.

"He runs," said one enthusiastic Irishman,
"like a leprechaun flittin' over the peat bogs
in the moonlight."

The only people who are less than enthusiastic about Ron are the record-minded customers who sit in the galleries for his races. They
object, sometimes grumpily and sometimes more
noisily, to his refusal to run against the clock.
Track fans set great store by records; nothing
excites them more than to see a new record
set. The race may be dull and one-sided, with
one man taking a big lead right at the begin-

ning and holding it all the way around, never being challenged. But if a record is broken, the spectators will go wild with excitement. By the same token, the most hotly contested duel of runners, ending in a tense breasting of the tape by two straining athletes only inches apart, may be greeted by only mild interest if no record is involved. And if the fans think the winner could easily have achieved a new record if he had bothered to try for it, they are likely to become downright hostile.

Ron Delany, who says he does not care about records and runs only to win his race, is very familiar with that hostility. He has been booed loud and often for stubbornly resisting the temptation to take out with all his might after a new record. "Records are only statistics," Delany says. "It's the race that matters. I think the sport of running is in the competition. And the competition isn't against the clock, it's against another human being. Now when I run against a man I get a kick out of it. But just trying to run against a stopwatch doesn't give me any enjoyment at all. The pleasure of running to me is not in making records but in winning races by beating the other man in a fair run.

"When I was eighteen, I was running for the Catholic University School in Dublin, and before a race I asked our moderator of athletics, Father Lonergan, if I should try to break the old record. I've never forgotten what he said to me. 'Don't do anything of the sort, Ronnie,' he said. 'Run to win your race, that's all.' I've followed that advice ever since."

It isn't, of course, that Ron has any phobia against running a race in record time. He will run as fast as he has to run to win, and if that involves putting a new set of figures in the record books, that's all right with him. In Compton, California, in the spring of 1956, he had to get under four minutes in order to beat Gunnar Nielsen of Denmark in a spectacular Invitational Mile. Nielsen ran such a powerful race, and had so much kick left at the finish, that Ron had to rocket across the finish line in 3:59 to edge in front of Nielsen, who was timed in 3:59.1. But his goal was to win the race, not to break four minutes.

The National AAU Mile at Madison Square Garden in February, 1958, which turned out to be one of Delany's finest indoor races, is a good example of the smiling Irishman's method of deciding how fast he will run by the pace that is set in each individual race. The tightly banked board track at the Garden is a difficult surface on which to find running room. The start is always crowded and there is considerable danger of unintentional tripping as the pack sprints for the first turn. On all the turns, for that matter, flying elbows are a hazard. So is the problem of deciding whether to let your chief rival set the pace or settle in comfortably behind you; either way, you have to worry that you may be giving him the advantage of initiative. That was exactly the dilemma Ron had to contend with in the AAU race, because the crack Hungarian miler, Istvan Rozsavolgyi, who always runs a pre-arranged race against the clock without regard for what his opponents are doing, was the man he had to contend with.

Delany's decision was to pay no attention to Rozsy, the newspaper writers' nickname for Rozsavolgyi. Ron, looking pale and fragile compared with the wiry Hungarian, glided easily into a place just a few feet off Phil Coleman's lead, and paid no attention at all to the fact that the first half was run in a slow 2:05.2. Rozsy, farther back, clearly was troubled by the dragging pace; it was as if he felt that he was off his timetable and had better do something soon to get back on it. He began to press forward, moving up through the pack in an effort to take the lead. Delany, meanwhile, was just coasting along in second place, conserving his energy for whatever challenges might lie ahead. When Rozsy's determined push carried him past both Delany and Coleman as they headed into the last quarter, Ron responded as his training and his instincts directed him to. He turned on the speed. It seemed quite a bit too early for the final sprint, but if Rozsy was going to try to run away with the race, he would have to give him a fight. Stubbornly, Ron lengthened his stride and ran headlong after the leader, passed him like the Twentieth Century Limited with an open throttle, and went on to win by twelve yards or more.

It wasn't the kind of race that Ron had intended to run, but it was the only kind of race that he could have run under the circumstances. A less adaptable runner would have been confused and routed; Delany, who pays no attention to pre-race plans, quarter times or problems of pace, simply obeyed his instincts and ran down the man who got in front of him. The fact that in doing so he sped through a

56.4 final quarter, and was clocked for the full mile in a sizzling 4:03.07, just one-tenth of a second short of the indoor record, meant nothing to him. He had won the race, he had left Rozsavolgyi gasping for breath in the stretch, and that was all that mattered.

It is clear to everyone who loves track and field that Ron's strange indifference to records is not an indifference to winning. He cares a great deal about winning. He made that clear in March of 1957 when he backed up Villanova's bid for the IC4A championship by an unprecedented and almost unbelievable "double" in the 1,000-yard and two-mile races. Running before a big crowd at Madison Square Garden, Ron took the 1,000 without any trouble, giving it just enough gas to fly home in front in the routine time of 2:14. The schedule of events allowed him just forty-eight minutes of rest before he had to jump off in the two-mile, a distance he had never run in competition in his life. What he did in that race will be remembered for a long time by those who saw it.

Alex Breckenridge of Villanova, an experienced two-miler, was running hard on the heels of the leader, Lew Stieglitz, of Connecticut. Delany was an arm's length behind Breckenridge, and most of the people in the gallery thought he looked tired. But with three laps to go, Ron showed signs of life. He appeared to be trying to urge Breckenridge on; for a while, he spurted in front of his teammate, as though to pull him along with him. Dropping behind again, he tried another trick: pulling abreast, he spanked Breckenridge smartly on the back-side, and only when Breck failed to respond did Ron take off by himself. But he did take off. The slim Irishman who had run a hard race less than an hour before quickened his stride and took off grimly after the pacemaker from Con-necticut. The crowd, alive to the sharp edge of competition, roared with excitement. Could Ron catch him?

When Stieglitz reached the mile-and-three-quarter marker, Delany was fifty yards behind.

With two laps to go, Ron was thirty yards behind, and gaining.

With the sound of the gun notifying the runners and the crowd that the last lap had begun, Ron had twenty yards to make up. He was running hard, giving it everything he had, and for once the Madison Square Garden fans were rooting him home. They whistled and shouted and stamped their feet as he flew into the last turn, collared the leader, passed him and swept on to a richly deserved eight-yard victory.

"I've never seen anything like it," Dan Ferris, the old man of the AAU said, emotionally. "He's the greatest ever. There's never been anybody like him."

Greg Rice, who was one of the greatest two-mile champions in track history, said, "Gunder Hagg was great, but he didn't have Delany's competitive heart. I once did a 58-second last quarter against Don Lash, but this fellow did it in 57, and he did it right after running a 2:14 thousand. I've never seen anything so exciting."

The Dublin boy with the old-fashioned bartender's haircut who caused all that commotion was born on March 6, 1935, in a small County Wicklow fishing village called Arklow. He lived there until he was five, when his father, Paddy, a customs inspector, was transferred to Dublin. Ron went first to the O'Connell School and then to the Catholic University School, where he showed great skill at tennis, Rugby football, field hockey and cricket, as well as track. It was while he was competing for Catholic University School as a half-miler that he was spotted by Fred Dwyer, intercollegiate mile champion at Villanova from 1951 to 1953, who happened to be in Dublin as a member of a touring AAU team. Dwyer talked seriously to Delany about the advantages of going to college in the United States, and Ron decided to give it a try. He entered Villanova in September, 1954, on an athletic scholarship, with the privilege of earning $5 a week spending money by directing traffic at the Sunday Masses at St. Thomas' Church.

Wherever and whenever Villanova's track coach, Jim (Jumbo) Elliott, asked him to run, Delany gave all that he had in him. In meet after meet, he smashed records and ran away with the competition. He loved to run. None of the other sports that he had tried had given him the pleasure and satisfaction that he got from running. "Track, and track alone," he said, "provides the opportunity to compete on an equal basis, man against man. In tennis, for example, there is a margin of error in a bad racket that gives one man an unfair advantage over another. There is an acquired technical skill essential in handling a weapon in many sports. If your grip is not proper, you're at a disadvantage. In Rugby, you depend upon the other fourteen men for success. In track, however, it is you, stripped down, all by yourself, against your opponents. Nobody brings any help or any weapons into the contest. You're on your own, against the field."

Delany ran fine races for Villanova in his college years, but it is safe to say that his greatest effort was the 1,500-meters in the 1956 Olympic Games at Melbourne. With the eyes of the whole world upon him, and the people of his own country pulling for him with all their strength, he came on from tenth place at the beginning of the last lap and sped over the red-brick cinders in the equivalent of a 3:58.2 mile as he raced to an Olympic 1,500-meter record of 3:41.2, winning the gold medal that was to mean so much to his countrymen.

Ron was on the outside when the race began, and he held his position somewhere between eighth and eleventh until the pack hit the last quarter. Then, as he told Dublin radioman Philip Green in an exclusive interview a few months later, he got a chance to move inside Gunnar Nielsen of Denmark, who was fading fast. "He could have helped me or he could have shut me out," Delany said, "but he let me run inside him and it gave me a great opportunity. We had about three hundred yards to go then, and after I passed Nielsen I moved on outside without having to worry about losing ground because there was nothing left but the straightaway and we all had to run the same exact distance there. I moved up slowly, and I was feeling pretty strong. John Landy was ahead of me but I got by him pretty easily and that left me in fourth place with about a hundred and eighty yards to go."

Delany had no way of knowing it at the time, but he had the race won right then. He had the momentum and none of his rivals could hold him off. He was full of running as he raced down the last hundred yards of the straightaway and broke the tape with his arms thrown out joyfully in the air, a picture that was reprinted in every newspaper in Ireland the next day.

One of the amazing things about the Olympic victory of the black-haired boy with the five-foot eleven-inch, 150-pound, greyhound build was that he had become the Olympic champion at the metric mile distance only a year and a half after he had run the mile for the first time in his life. That was on his first visit home to Dublin after his freshman year at

Villanova. He had been only a half-miler that first year in college, and he was doubtful when the home folks pleaded with him to have a go at the Irish mile record. "I couldn't disappoint them, now, could I?" he says, remembering. And, of course, he couldn't. So he not only ran the distance but he also broke the national record with a spectacular 4:05.8, the only time in any sort of competition he ever deliberately has gone out after a record. He couldn't have picked a better time.

Whether or not he ever will break his rule and try for a new record in the United States, no one knows. The chances are that he won't, but even the most stubborn Irishman occasionally changes his mind. Ron tells a story about himself which illustrates that point exactly. "Everything I am," he said, "I owe to my coach at Villanova, Jim Elliott. No coach ever worked harder or more patiently with a runner than he did with me. The one thing he just couldn't hammer into my thick head was a way for me to improve my arm action.

"But when I got to Australia for the Olympic Games, John Landy said to me, 'Ron, you're going to win.' 'Please God,' I told him, 'I hope I do.' 'You will,' he said. 'All you've got to do is learn to relax and improve your arm action.'

"Well, when Landy said exactly what Elliott had been saying, all of Jim's advice came right back into my mind. Jim had been right about everything he had tried to teach me, and obviously I'd been ignoring one of the soundest pieces of advice he had given me. Anyway, I went to work immediately on my arm action, and the results speak for themselves."

He didn't lose the touch when he got back to school, either. At one stretch of his intercollegiate career, Ron chalked up twenty-four consecutive victories in indoor mile races, a mark of achievement which will stand nicely until some future young Mercury does it one or two better. His tremendous running in the relay and half-mile races helped mightily to bring victory to Villanova in the 1958 Intercollegiates. In the 37th annual NCAA individual track and field championships at UCLA in the spring of '58, Ron scored another of his famous doubles, this time running off with the 880 and the mile. His exciting performance in the mile lowered Wes Santee's five-year-old NCAA record from 4:03.7 to 4:03.5. In the 880, running with less than half an hour's rest, he was last in the field of nine until he poured on the speed in the homestretch to win in the excellent time of 1:48.6 before more than 16,000 wildly cheering spectators.

Even when he finished a loser in a big race, as he did at Dublin in August, 1958, a few months after his graduation from college, Ron showed clearly that he was a runner of championship caliber. With almost 20,000 Irishmen looking on that day, he took third place in one of the greatest mile races of running history. All the first five placers ran the distance in less than four minutes, and Australia's Herb Elliott, the winner, set a new world record with an almost unbelievable mark of 3:54.5. Merv Lincoln, another Australian, was second in 3:55.9; Ron, the hope of the Irish, was third in 3:57.5; Murray Halberg of New Zealand was fourth in the same time recorded by Delany, 3:57.5; and Albert Thomas of Australia was fifth in 3:58.6. The lap times for the fantastic foot race were 58 seconds for the first quarter, 1:58 for the half, and 2:59 for three quarters. It was the first time five men had broken four minutes in the same race, and nobody who saw the race is likely ever to forget it. Even though he could do no better than third, Ron was exceedingly proud of his part in it.

His countrymen, aware that a man who can run the mile in 3:57.5 undoubtedly can run it even faster, are confident that Delany's greatest feats still lie ahead of him. He is a young man yet and he will be only twenty-four when the 1960 Olympic Games are held in Rome. No one can say with any confidence that he already has reached his peak. On the contrary, the chances seem good that he will do considerably better in Rome than he did in Melbourne. He is learning more about the job of running all the time, and he is growing to like it more all the time, too.

"Running the mile is a real thrill," Ron says. "It's not so long a race that it can become boring, nor is it too short. But there's plenty of excitement, right from the start. Right from the gun, you get the smooth striding of the runners and the positioning of the field. Then, in the middle laps, there's the maintenance of the pace, the steady running as you watch your opponents carefully. Then someone moves up, and then someone else, and suddenly you're only a lap from the finish! Then there's the mad burst for the tape, a complete element of excitement. There's really nothing quite like it in sport."

Ron is too modest to say so, but the rewards of his remarkable talent have been exciting, too. The fine education he has received in the United States, the trips he has made all over the world, and, above all, the wonderful tributes he has received in his own country—all these things he has been given because of the way he has worked to develop his God-given gifts of speed and endurance.

Ron expects to spend much of his time in the United States in the years ahead. With his Irish brogue on his tongue, his Miraculous Medal and green scapular around his neck, and a pile of letters from home on the dresser in his room, he is taking graduate courses at Villanova and working part-time for Irish Air Lines. When his studies finally are completed, he expects to go to work full-time for the Air Lines, and he hopes the company will find his services useful long after he has ceased to be able to run a mile in four minutes.

No matter how much time he spends in the United States, Ron Delany's home will always be Ireland. He won't soon forget the time he was taken to the Lord Mayor's mansion in

Dublin, and the police had to clear a path for him through the admiring crowd gathered outside, so that he could climb the steps and shake hands with Robert Briscoe, the Lord Mayor himself. "It is my great privilege," said Mr. Briscoe firmly, "to be in office when a Dublin citizen has brought so much credit not only to Dublin but to Ireland by his wonderful accomplishment. It gives me the greatest of pleasure, Ronnie Delany, to extend to you the warmest congratulations of all our citizens."

Nor will he forget visiting the crippled children at St. Mary's Hospital in Cappagh, making the rounds from bed to bed, shaking hands with the children, grinning in a friendly way at the little paper hats the Sisters of the hospital had made for them in honor of the occasion. He was beginning to understand that being a national sports hero carries its obligations and responsibilities as well as its pleasures.

The chances are that Ron always will remember best the good times at home, in Ireland, for he is a home boy through and through. He once told a New York reporter that, when he is away, all he has to do is close his eyes and he can see, in his mind, Phoenix Park in Dublin; St. Stephen's Green, at the top of Grafton Street; the wide bridge that carries O'Connell Street across the Liffey River; and the General Post Office which became the headquarters of the Easter Rebellion against the British way back in 1916.

Standing in a New York hotel room, he watched the rain beating down against the windows, and said, out of the depths of his homesickness, "This is one of those times when Dubliners like to say, 'It's a fine, soft night, thanks be to God.'

"Truthfully," Ron added, "there are no bad days in Dublin."

If all Dubliners are like Ronald Michael Delany, it is easy to see how that must be so.

Chapter Six

EDDIE ARCARO: BIG MAN IN THE SADDLE

In boxing, there was only one Jack Dempsey. In football, there was only one Red Grange. In baseball, there was only one Ty Cobb. In tennis, there was only one Bill Tilden. And in horseracing, sometimes known as the sport of kings, there is only one Eddie Arcaro.

Eddie Arcaro is a millionaire. He became one by winning more than 4,000 horse races worth almost $23,000,000 in purses. Since the jockey customarily is paid ten per cent of his stakes winnings, you can see that Eddie's share of this huge total has added up to well over two million dollars. He has won the Kentucky Derby, the most famous of all American races, five times—more often than any other jockey in history. He is an inspiration to every boy whose small stature may cause him to worry that he will never be able to amount to anything in a world dominated by bigger men. Eddie is only five feet, three inches tall, and he weighs only 108 pounds, but in wealth and position and the respect of his peers he takes second place to nobody in the sports world. He's an acknowledged champion.

Arcaro is so highly respected for his ability to get the most out of a running horse that many people will pick his mount to win a race simply because he is riding it. In a sport in which people generally back up their opinions with large sums of money, that's a handsome tribute. Coupled with it is another prized tribute. If an owner or trainer has a horse which he thinks has a chance of winning a big race, he invariably looks first for Arcaro to climb into the saddle. He may settle for Willie Shoemaker or Johnny Longden or Conn McCreary, but if he can have the man he wants, he gets

Eddie Arcaro. And finally, among his fellow jockeys, the men he has to ride against every day in the week, Arcaro is universally regarded as the king of them all. "He's the greatest," young Jimmy Del Vecchio said in the jockeys' room at Belmont one day recently. "There's nobody even close to him."

People who single him out as the best of his craft probably would agree with Eddie that it's impossible to pick any one of his thousands of winning races as his best. It might not be too far from wrong, however, to put the spotlight on the Belmont Stakes of 1952, when Eddie rode a horse named One Count to a truly spectacular victory. Two horses in that race figured to be better than Arcaro's; both Armageddon and Blue Man were favored by the handicappers. Arcaro himself said, in the jockeys' room the day before the race, "There isn't a boy in this room who wouldn't like to be riding Blue Man. I sure wish I was going to."

But that didn't prevent him from making an all-out effort to win with the horse he had been assigned. "The two horses I had to watch," Eddie said, "were Blue Man and Armageddon. When we were going up the backstretch, I was right behind Armageddon. For a while there, I thought he was going to bolt, and I took my horse back in a hurry for fear I'd climb right up on him. We were running along the rail, and when Ray York, who was on Armageddon, got him straightened out, I moved up alongside of him. I knew he didn't like to run on the rail, so I kept him there."

That took care of Armageddon's chances and enabled Arcaro to devote his full attention to Blue Man, the favorite. Blue Man was a come-from-behind horse that liked to wait until the last minute to pour it on. Furthermore, he was being ridden by Conn McCreary, a jockey who is famous for liking to come from the back of the pack down the homestretch. In this race, though, contrary to his custom, McCreary had Blue Man right up among the leaders, a close third. "I didn't know what he was doing up there," Eddie said. "I kept waiting for him to fall back. When he didn't, I figured I could beat him from there because it looked as if he was making his big move. I was sure that if he was making his run from there, my horse could outspeed him."

Eddie urged his horse on with all his skill and guile. He passed the leader, Sub Fleet, and he held his surging racer in front all the way down under the finish wire, even though Blue Man came on with a tremendous rush and challenged furiously for the lead in the last fifty yards. It was a great exhibition by a real master.

Eddie Arcaro is in the habit of giving his horses masterful rides. He has been doing it for well over twenty years, and even though he celebrated his forty-third birthday in February of 1959, he has made it clear that, unless he is unlucky enough to get hurt, he hopes to keep on riding for a few more years. "I'd like to," he says candidly, "because after I quit I'll just be another small man, instead of Eddie Arcaro the jockey, and I'm in no hurry for that to happen."

It isn't likely ever to happen because the man who has won more Kentucky Derbies than any other jockey is already an enduring legend in the sport. He won't soon be forgotten. The people will remember, for one thing, the terrific ride he gave Lawrin to win his first Derby way back in 1938. Lawrin was an outsider in the big race at Churchill Downs, a 10–1 shot in the pre-race calculations. The favorite was Belair's Fighting Fox and the second choice was Calumet's Bull Lea, with Hal Price Headley's

Menow also heavily backed by the horse-wise
Kentucky hardboots. But Ben Jones, an un-
known horse trainer from Parnell, Missouri,
who was to become famous as the trainer of
Calumet's multi-million-dollar stable of champions, was sure he had a strong contender in
Lawrin. He made a big bet on him himself, and
he was a happy man when his skillful jockey,
using his powerful wrists and arms to the fullest, rocketed past the more highly touted horses
to win going away and return $19.20 for a
two-dollar investment. That was the race that
made Eddie Arcaro famous, and he has built
upon his fame ever since.

Even Arcaro's mistakes have become part of
the legend. Take, for instance, the Kentucky
Derby of 1942. Eddie was the regular rider for
the wealthy Greentree Stable that year, and
Greentree had two hot candidates for the race,
Devil Diver and Shut Out. As the stable's No.
1 rider, Arcaro had the right to choose his
mount. He picked Devil Diver, and his choice
has been cited ever since as the classic example
of how little anyone, even the jockeys, knows
about the business of picking winners at the
race track. For, with all the information he had
at his disposal, Eddie chose the wrong horse.

Shut Out, with Wayne Wright in the saddle, won in a gallop; Devil Diver finished so far back that it didn't look as if he even cared.

In Eddie's second Derby victory, aboard Whirlaway in 1941, he gave the late-running Calumet star a slick, professional ride to come from behind and run away with the wreath of roses that is the Derby winner's badge of victory. He came back to Churchill Downs, in later years, to win with Hoop Junior, with Citation and Hill Gail. Of them all, Eddie is least likely to forget the nerve-tingling 1948 Derby when he made it home in first place with Citation, the first horse ever to win more than a million dollars at the race track.

Eddie wasn't so sure he wanted to be on Citation in that race. It was another one of those stablemate situations. Calumet also had entered a speedy colt named Coaltown, which had broken a hatful of track records in Florida and Kentucky with such ease and power that one groom said of him, "That Coaltown is no race horse, he's a freak." Eddie heard the stable gossip about the speed horse and finally was moved to mention his uncertainty to the boss, Ben Jones. "Are you sure," he asked the trainer, "I'm not on the wrong horse?"

"Eddie," Jones said, "if I thought Coaltown would win this Derby, you'd be on him."

That was good enough for Eddie, and he listened carefully to the strategy Jones laid down for the race. The idea was for Coaltown to take the lead at the start and stretch it as far as he could go. The stable had no intention of ordering Newbold Pierson, who was up on Coaltown, to pull back on his horse, and it would be strictly up to Arcaro to catch him.

In his autobiography, *I Ride To Win*, Eddie said, "As I sat there in the starting gate on the horse that almost everybody expected me to bring home in front, I was obsessed with one question: When should I go after Coaltown? Everybody conceded that he would have the early speed and would be out there setting the pace. With only six horses in the race, I shouldn't run into any trouble at the start. My job was simply to open up the throttle at exactly the right point in the race."

Eddie had good reason to feel a gnawing sense of responsibility. Ben Jones hadn't minced any words in giving his opinion of Citation. "The horse Citation can't run down hasn't been born," Jones told his friends, and his friends told their friends and on and on until Arcaro was placed in the position of being astride a red-hot favorite with everything to lose and nothing much to gain. If he won, he was only doing the expected. If he lost, he was a bum.

As a matter of fact, Eddie didn't even stand to enrich himself financially by winning. Citation was supposed to have been ridden by jockey Al Snider, but Snider was drowned on March 8, 1948, on a fishing trip off the Florida Keys. When Ben Jones asked Arcaro to take over for Snider in the Derby, Eddie said he would be glad to, on one condition. He insisted that Snider's widow be given half of whatever amount he earned for riding in the race. It was a heartwarmingly generous gesture, one that the other jockeys never have forgotten, and it is one of the many reasons why they never seem to resent Arcaro's rapidly accumulating wealth.

Jones's plan of battle worked just as though it all had been rehearsed. Before the pack had sprinted an eighth of a mile, Coaltown was six lengths in front and going like a house afire. "I stayed in second position down the backstretch," Eddie said, "and Coaltown was still eating up the ground, maybe four lengths in front, as we came to the far turn. Then I asked Citation for it, and we began to move. It was as though his legs were made of steel springs. He actually bounded after Coaltown. At the three-sixteenths pole, we drew even. Bending down and clucking to him, I could feel him continue to surge ahead with that blazing speed of his, and at the end he was going away by three and a half lengths. Coaltown was second and My Request was third."

Eddie often has said that if Coaltown ever was going to beat Citation, it would have had to be that day. But after Citation had picked up the front runner and stowed him away in his pocket, everybody knew that Coaltown never would see the day he could match strides with his great stablemate. Old Ben Jones had called the turn perfectly.

Citation earned $83,400 for his victory, and Arcaro's ten per cent was worth $8,340. Half of that went, as he had directed, to Mrs. Al Snider.

That day Eddie didn't have the problem he had on one frustrating day at the races which resulted in one of the most widely repeated stories about him. It seems that he was up on a run-of-the-mill horse whose trainer, for some wildly optimistic reason, thought he had a chance to win. Before the race, as they stood in the paddock, the trainer gave Arcaro detailed instructions on just how to go out of the gate, how to rate the horse around the first turn and along the backstretch, exactly when to make his move and how to come on down the last stretch. When the race was over, and Eddie's mount had finished dead last, the trainer approached him and berated him for not following orders. "Didn't I tell you to come out of the gate fast and then rate him back and then make your move at the head of the backstretch and come on to win?" he demanded angrily.

"What was I supposed to do," Arcaro shot back, "leave the horse?"

Eddie has been working at his trade ever since he was in his teens. He was born in Cincinnati but grew up in Newport, Kentucky, where his father, Pasquale Arcaro, had a glass and chinaware business. Both of Eddie's parents were small in stature and little Eddie weighed only eighty-two pounds when he entered high school. Unhappy in school, because the other boys made fun of him all the time, he began playing hooky as often as he dared. Sometimes he went to the Highland Country Club to make a few dollars by caddying, and sometimes he obeyed an instinctive longing and visited the Latonia race track, spending the money his father gave him for lunch on long, four-hour round-trip streetcar rides to get there and back. Once, he admits, he stayed out of school for forty straight days before school officials caught up to him and made him bring in his mother and father for a talk.

Eddie's insistence that all he wanted was to be a jockey impressed not only his parents but also the school principal. All parties concerned made a deal with him; he could withdraw from school for a year and concentrate on learning how to ride. If, at the end of a year, he hadn't made noticeable progress, he would have to give it up and come back to school. Eddie thought it was a wonderfully fair proposition and he accepted it gladly.

For a while, it didn't look as if Eddie was going to make it anywhere except back to the classroom. It wasn't that he didn't work hard. Tom McCaffray, a well-to-do Cincinnati shoe manufacturer, gave him a job in his stable, and Eddie swept out the stables, cleaned the equipment, patiently walked horses to cool them off after their workouts, and, finally, got his chance to ride a few exercise gallops on his own. He didn't impress Mr. McCaffray. "If this boy ever makes a rider," McCaffray told Pasquale Arcaro one day, "we'll have snow right here in July." But young Eddie was cocky as well as stubborn. "It could be," he said swiftly. "We had a little hail just the other day." And he stuck to his riding, once even getting a mount of his own in a cheap claiming race. "I lost my cap and the color came out of my pants," he says, grinning. "I did everything but fall off the horse."

When he was fifteen, Eddie took off for Agua Caliente, Mexico. He went from stable to stable pleading for a chance to ride, and finally he ran into a horseman named Clarence Davison who took pity on him. Davison did more than give Eddie an opportunity to learn his trade; he literally taught it to him. "I want you to ride this quarter in fifty seconds," Davison would tell him, holding a stopwatch in his hand. "And I don't mean fifty-one seconds or forty-nine seconds. I mean exactly fifty seconds." It was up to the skinny, hawk-nosed boy to count off the seconds and pace the horse accordingly. As a result of that early training, Eddie's sense of timing is so exquisite today that around the tracks he is known as "Mister Stopwatch."

Davison taught him all the tricks of the trade, how to break fast out of the starting gate, how to protect himself against the punching, kicking and rough-riding tactics of jockeys who didn't care how they won so long as they won, and how to pick out a hole in the charging pack of horses and glide through it safely into the daylight ahead. "I'll never forget Mr. Davison," Eddie says with emotion. "I did everything wrong, but he stayed with me. When I think of how many races I lost for him, I know it's a wonder he didn't throw me out on my ear." Davison not only didn't throw Eddie out, he and his wife actually took him into their home and virtually adopted him.

Eddie figures he must have ridden in almost a hundred races before he scored his first victory, and, even now, more than 4,000 wins later, he still remembers the horse and the date. The horse's name was Eagle Bird, and it was a claiming race at Agua Caliente on January 14, 1932. Things were so tough for Davison that Eddie's boss had to leave Eagle Bird behind to cover the bills he owed when he shipped his string of horses out of Caliente and headed for

Sportsman's Park in Chicago. In a way, it probably was a lucky thing for Arcaro that his boss was so poor. If Davison had had more money, he might never have stuck so long with the awkward apprentice. As it was, the owner-trainer needed the boy, and because it served his own purposes, he kept teaching him everything he knew about the business. Long after Eddie had begun riding for money, he used to spend his evenings sitting on a bale of hay in the barn, his reins rigged to a bucket on the floor, practicing his hand-riding technique. It was hard work, and tiring, but Eddie came out of it a wise and skilled jockey.

It was in Chicago that he first began to show his ability. In one stretch, he rode fourteen winners in one week. He was beginning to learn how to save ground with his horse by hugging the rail at every opportunity and not allowing himself to be forced outside where he had to cover more yards to the finish line, how to pace his mount, when and how to take the whip to the horse, and how to watch every inch of the track for the best footing. When Davison took him from Chicago to New Orleans, he was the leading rider with forty-three winners. People were beginning to notice him, and to talk about him approvingly, and it came as no great surprise when the mighty Calumet Farm approached Davison and offered him $5,000 for Eddie's services as a contract rider. Partly for his own sake, but mostly for Eddie's, Davison accepted.

With his new status as a regular rider for one of the sport's most famous and most respected stables, Arcaro got a salary of $650 per month. It was, for him, untold wealth. In addition, he had a handsome stake from his years with Davison. "Every time I got any money for riding a horse for somebody else," Eddie says, "Mr. Davison made me give it to him. He always wrote the amount down carefully in a little black book he kept in his pocket. When I left him to go with Calumet, he brought out the book and added it up and it came to $3,500. He went to the bank and drew it out and gave it to me all in one lump. Nobody ever was treated any better than he treated me. Believe me, there have been lots of times since when I wished I still had him around."

In those first years, Eddie acquired a reputation as something of a roughneck. If anybody elbowed him flying down the homestretch, he elbowed right back—and maybe a little harder. He served out more than his share of suspensions. But once he gained confidence in himself and grew up enough to realize that it was far better to win within the rules than outside of them, he forgot about the rough stuff and concentrated on his riding. He became a much better jockey for it, and the clean way he rides his races today probably has a lot to do with his reputation among his fellow jockeys. Most of them pick him as an even better rider than the famous Earl Sande, the kingpin of the 1920's and the man of whom Damon Runyon wrote: "Gimme a handy guy like Sande, bootin' those winners home." Sande was a tough man in the tight spots on the turns, and he isn't remembered too fondly by a lot of the old-timers.

With Arcaro, it's different. Half a dozen years ago a reporter was talking to Gordon Glisson, then a leading apprentice at Santa Anita, and Glisson spoke warmly of Eddie's willingness to go out of his way to help the younger riders. "I've been riding only about a year," Glisson said, "so Eddie kind of takes me under his wing. It started up at Tanforan last December. I asked him to show me how he switches his whip from one hand to the other so fast, and one day when we were going to the post he called over to me, 'Hey, watch this!' Eddie does it so fast you can hardly follow his hands. He saw I was a righthander and couldn't hit with my left hand, so he kept on showing me until I finally got the idea. He's a great guy, believe me."

Another instance cited by Glisson involved a race in which his horse was pinned against the rail as the field charged down the backstretch. All of a sudden an inexperienced jockey on a wild horse began to move in on him. With no place to go, Glisson thought sure he was headed for a crash against the rail. Seeing what was happening, Arcaro, a length or so behind, urged his mount up the middle and forced the veering horse back to the center of the track. He held him there until Glisson had a chance to pull out of the hole and regain running room. The maneuver meant that Arcaro was boxed in; he had sacrificed his own chances of winning the race, and Glisson went on to take it handily.

"After it was over," Glisson said, "Eddie told me something I've never forgotten and I hope I never will. 'Remember,' he said, 'if you give the other rider a break, he'll give you one when you need it.'"

Eddie Arcaro has won so many horse races that they all seem to run together in the minds of the enthusiasts who follow the sport. Big ones and little ones, he has been in there holding a tight rein on his mount, looking for a hole to shoot through, clicking off the seconds in his mind and waiting for just the right moment to ask the horse for everything he's got in the big run for all the money.

Bill Corum, the famous sportswriter who was president of Churchill Downs and who put on racing's greatest show, the Kentucky Derby, every year, remembered an unimportant race Eddie rode one Saturday afternoon in 1947 at Jamaica. "When Arcaro came up to the last race after riding four winners in a row," Corum said, "it looked to me like a good spot to make a bet on him. Knowing Eddie, I figured he could see that headline in the papers, 'Five in a Row for Arcaro,' as clearly as anybody else around there could see it. He had to have the horse, of course. That's the first rule. The horse must carry the jockey or the stewards won't let you in the race. But some of those who watched that seventh race

at Jamaica last Saturday may remember, as I
do, that with his mount, Bright Sword, four
lengths in front of the field with only fifty
yards to go, Eddie rode as furiously as if it was
a photo finish. He didn't just win it, he won
it by six lengths and heading for the barn. He's
a competitor, that boy, as well as a good rider
and an excellent judge of horses."

Many another racing fan remembers the
magnificent ride Eddie gave Nashua in the
match race with Swaps at Washington Park in
Chicago on August 31, 1955. Nashua, the pride
of the Belair Stud stable, had been beaten by
the California speed horse, Swaps, in the Kentucky Derby. Public opinion brought about the
historic match race between the two to settle,
once and for all, the question of which horse
was the three-year-old champion of the season.
Ben Lindheimer, the operator of Washington
Park, posted a prize purse of $100,000 to the
winner, and 36,000 lovers of fine horseflesh
crowded into the track to see the excitement.

Because Nashua was known as a late running
horse and Swaps as a sprinter possessed of blinding speed, it was generally expected that Swaps
would break fast out of the gate and take the
lead and hold it until, in the stretch, Nashua

would ask the big question and the race would be decided in the last yards. But the men in Nashua's camp didn't see it that way. William Woodward, the horse's owner, and Sunny Jim Fitzsimmons, his trainer, quietly suggested to Arcaro that he get to the front right off the bat, if possible—and that he should forget the "if possible" part. Their strategy was to catch Swaps and his jockey, Willie Shoemaker, by surprise, and run the western horse down without delay.

When the bell rang to open the starting gate at 5:18 P.M., Eddie Arcaro was, in the words of one reporter, "a fighting, bellowing cavalryman. Ahead of him lay a mile and a quarter of combat terrain. Beyond that lay a check for $100,000, a tenth of it for the winning jockey, not to mention a gold cup for the mantelpiece back home in Rockville Centre, Long Island. But more important than all this was the prestige which Eddie Arcaro had built up as the foremost race rider of his generation, the smartest, the trickiest, the headiest—and the hungriest when the heavy green bills are waiting to be picked up in the winner's circle."

As the barrier was sprung, Arcaro spurred Nashua out of the gate like a thunderbolt. The track was slightly muddy, with two good running strips visible in the turf, one leading out of stall No. 3 and the other out of stall No. 5. Arcaro, intent upon saving as much ground as possible by running close to the rail, beat Shoemaker and Swaps to the inside path. To all intents and purposes, the race was won right then and there. Shoemaker had to stay outside, which was exactly where Arcaro wanted him to be, and that's where Arcaro kept him all through the race.

They galloped furiously into the clubhouse turn, with Eddie holding Shoemaker and his mount well outside and thus forcing him to run a longer race. Swaps made the first of three hard runs at Nashua, but Nashua stood him off like a champion. At the top of the backstretch, with the two sleek horses racing stride for stride, a length apart, in as pretty a duel as anyone ever saw on a race track, Swaps tried for the third and last time to run down the horse he had beaten in Kentucky. Neither Nashua nor Arcaro was having any. Eddie drew his horse out to a lead of a length and a half, then three lengths, four, and finally six, and that's the way it was at the finish. The master jockey had done it again.

It is impossible to overestimate the importance of the role the jockey plays in a race. True, the horse has to carry him around the track, but it is the jockey who does the thinking, not the horse. "Actually," Eddie says, "of all the horses I ride, I'd say about seventy per cent of them don't really care about winning. They don't like to run out by themselves, or they don't like moving up in the pack and getting dirt kicked in their faces, or they don't like something else. But when you get a horse like that, you try to fool him. You try, for instance, to time it so that he's just breaking through at the finish. A lot of horses—you can look them up in the charts—run second lots of times, but they don't win. People bet on them; the jockeys call them 'sucker horses.' But I won a race this afternoon on a horse like that. I just got her in front and made up my mind I was going to keep her there as long as she'd stay. And she stayed. The next time, maybe, she won't stay. When you're riding cheap horses like that, you try to steal a race. You get out there and go. You know, like stealing home in a close ball game."

A good jockey is much more than a rider; he is an athlete. He has to have perfect balance, strong legs to sit properly on the horse and grip him tightly with knees and shins, and powerful wrists to control the reins and the horse's head. Nor is brute strength the whole story when it comes to hand-riding. "A jockey," Arcaro says, "has got to have the touch in his hands, the feel. Everything goes between the jockey's hands and the horse's mouth. That's the contact between them. He's got to have a touch like a musician's."

Eddie won't say so because he doesn't like to boast, but it is obvious that a winning jockey also has to have enough courage to supply a platoon of infantrymen. When the horses, weighing twelve hundred pounds apiece and running full tilt, jam into each other on the turns, and the jockey looks down and sees all those flying hooves waiting to chew him up like a matchstick if he is knocked off his precarious perch, it takes nerve to force his way through to the lead.

Eddie tried to sum up the requirements of his profession. "A lot of it," he said, "is strength, because you're pushing a lot of horse out there. A lot of it is learning. There's no such thing as a natural jockey. I don't think I know a thing about riding that I didn't have to be taught. But I guess the biggest thing of all is that you've got to want to win. I've seen jockeys who lacked a lot of skills who won a lot of races just because they wanted to win so badly. Maybe they can't keep it up, maybe they get beaten down physically. But for a while, until the punishment catches up to them, they can be great, just because they don't even consider losing."

America's greatest jockey has money in the bank and business holdings that will maintain him and his family in comfort if he never rides another horse race. He and his wife, Ruth, and their children, Carolyn and Eddie Jr., live in a handsome English-style home. Some of the most famous figures in public life are his friends. By any standard, Eddie Arcaro is a thumping success, and he has made it because he has the three things a man in his occupation must have—skill, courage, and the will to win. In any occupation, that combination is unbeatable.

Chapter Seven

"B" STANDS FOR BELIVEAU AND BEST

The best hockey player in the world today is Jean Beliveau of the Montreal Canadiens, and he isn't even the most famous player on his own team. That honor unquestionably belongs to Maurice Richard, the incomparable Rocket, the highest scorer in the history of the game and one of the most colorful performers ever to send a hockey crowd into hysterics. But whether or not Beliveau ever manages to catch up to the older Richard's scoring records, the managers, coaches, players, writers and fans all agree that he is the most skillful man in the game today.

Le Gros Bill, "Big Bill," as the French-Canadians call him, plays hockey the way Joe Di-Maggio used to play baseball. He is big—six feet three inches tall—and powerful, but he glides around the ice with the gracefulness of a small man. He shoots with such deceptive ease that you don't realize how hard he has driven the puck until it flies past the goal-keeper's desperate lunge and buries itself quivering in the net. He has such an instinctive feel for the skills of the game that he makes the most difficult plays look routine. As a result, he isn't noticed nearly so much as a player who has to work twice as hard to accomplish half as much. But the professionals know what he is doing out there, and gradually their admiration for Beliveau's great talent has come to be shared by the more emotional fans in the stands. They know that when they watch Big Bill swoop down the ice at the point of the Cana-diens' famous power play, and get off that wicked slap shot that is by far the hottest shot in hockey, they are seeing one of the great ones of all hockey history.

"He is the most polished hockey player there ever was," his boss, Frank Selke, the managing director of the Canadiens, says. "That's why he drew such fantastic crowds when he was an amateur in Quebec. You have to go all the way back to Lester Patrick, in another generation, to find one like him. There are others as effective as he is, but none as smooth and easy."

Because he doesn't have an explosive temperament like the mercurial Richard, and doesn't get involved in a steady stream of feuds and fights and other embroilments, Beliveau has had to depend solely on his magnificent abilities to command the attention of the crowd. He doesn't need anything more. There have been critics along the line who have complained that he lacked this or that vital ingredient of true greatness, but they always have been disproved by his effortless performances. Some have claimed, for example, that Beliveau doesn't have the blinding, sprinting speed of all-time centers like Syl Apps of the Maple Leafs. But Lynn Patrick, head man of the Boston Bruins, quickly disposes of that argument.

"We were playing the Canadiens one night," Patrick said, "and Milt Schmidt picked up a loose puck behind our own net and started for the opposite end of the rink. This Beliveau kid came around the net about ten yards behind Milt. It looked like strictly no contest because Schmidt was one of the fastest men in the league, especially on a breakaway play like that. But Beliveau caught him before he got to the Canadiens' blue line, reached out and just calmly snatched the puck off his stick. Believe me, Milt was the most surprised man in the place."

Others said grumpily that even if he did have all the skills, Beliveau just didn't have the competitive spirit to make the most of them. It's not only that he doesn't get into any fights, they complained, but, even worse, he lets everybody push him around.

There was some merit to this criticism. Jean hadn't had to contend with much rough stuff during his days as a star in the amateur league, and he wasn't prepared for the hammer-and-tongs way the boys went at the game in the big league. There somebody will try to knock down a player every time he skates toward the mouth of the goal, and body-checking often includes a wayward stick in the ribs or on the top of the head. At first, Beliveau tried to ignore the villains. But, as so often happens, his attitude was interpreted by the roughnecks as an invitation to pile on. In his first two seasons with the Canadiens, Beliveau submitted almost without protest to a fearful pummeling. The word flew around the league that the big fellow wouldn't cross-check, wouldn't trade a stick in the stomach for a stick in the stomach, and wouldn't even fight back if you took a punch at him.

"I always used to wonder why Maurice Richard had so many fights," Jean said. "But I found out. They won't leave him alone. Everybody clutches him, holds him illegally, waylays him when he tries to break loose. If he submits for a while, it gets worse. So he has to fight back. He does it to keep them from taking too many liberties, and I had to do the same thing. I had to let them know that I would protect myself."

There is no doubt in anybody's mind these days that Jean will do exactly that. He never will be known as a hothead or a troublemaker, because that simply is not his nature, but neither will anyone ever again make the mistake of thinking that Big Bill is a pushover for bullying tactics. He will cross sticks with anybody who tries to rough him up, and he is so astonishingly strong that few men in their right minds care to tangle with him.

Step by step, therefore, Jean has in just a few years established himself as the game's shining symbol of skill, the complete hockey player. Of course, a whole lifetime of apprenticeship to the sport lies behind him. In Three Rivers, the French-Canadian town in the province of Quebec where Jean Beliveau was born, the kids play hockey on the frozen ponds and lakes until their ears and noses and cheeks are bright red with the cold. Even when the drifting snow piles deep on the ice, they borrow shovels from their fathers and brooms from their mothers and clear off enough space for at least a compressed version of the game. They play from eight in the morning until six in the evening, taking only the briefest of rest periods for a lunch that usually consists only of a half-frozen sandwich brought to the lake in a paper bag and always eaten with the skates still on. By the time these boys grow to be sturdy teen-agers, they are experienced hockey players. "You keep playing and practicing and shooting," Jean says. "That's the only way to make it. And if you want to get to be better than the others, you really have to work extra hard at it, conditioning yourself and learning as much as you can."

Jean learned. He played all week long, and every Sunday he took time out to go watch the highly organized amateur teams play. He would study the big boys intently, following their every move with eyes that missed nothing and a mind that retained everything he saw.

When Jean's father, Arthur Beliveau, a foreman with a water and power company, moved the family to Victoriaville, the boy progressed to playing with a few of the town teams and with his school team. When he was fifteen, one of the Brothers at the school invited a Montreal scout to come and see him play. The visitor needed only one look to know he wanted Jean's signature on a contract to play with the Junior Canadiens. Jean signed, although his father was opposed to the idea of his playing anywhere except in his own town. Mr. Beliveau's sensible theory was that the boy ought to finish his basic schooling before he began traveling around the country playing hockey.

Partly because of the father's attitude, and partly because a promoter agreed to sponsor a fast amateur team in Victoriaville if Jean could

be made available to play, the Canadiens released him, on condition that he would revert
to their control at the end of the year. When
the new Victoriaville team collapsed from lack
of support, the Canadiens wanted Jean to come
back to their organization. But they didn't act
fast enough. Representatives of the Quebec
Citadelles, a junior amateur team in the big
city, talked Mr. Beliveau into letting Jean play
for them at the unheard-of sum of $125 per
week. In addition to the large salary, which
made the $25–$35 pay checks distributed by the
Canadiens to their juniors look like peanuts, the
Citadelles offered the inducement that Jean
would be allowed to play a number of games
right in Victoriaville. The Canadiens weren't
happy about losing him, but they were unwilling to risk a widespread salary revolt in the
ranks by paying Jean the kind of money he
was getting from the Citadelles. They did, of
course, still have clear-cut rights to his services
as a professional, if and when he should ever
decide to turn pro. The Canadiens' decision
to let Jean go didn't seem to be a terribly
important one at the time, but it assumed quite
different proportions two years later when the
youngster graduated from the junior class and

began to play with the Quebec Aces in senior amateur competition.

The Aces played in a brand-new $3,500,000 arena that seated 12,500 people who paid good prices to watch their favorites in action. Before more than a few weeks of his first season had gone by, Beliveau was their favorite of favorites. They gave him the nickname *Le Gros Bill* from a popular song of the time about a handsome cowboy who won the beautiful Pamela from the bad cowboy named Joe. So great was their affection for Beliveau that they instantly identified him in their minds with Big Bill, the hero of the song that was on everybody's lips. Big Bill he has been ever since.

Amateur hockey, which really isn't amateur at all, but is called that simply to distinguish it from the professional game, never has known a hero like Beliveau. Not more than a handful of the stars of the National Hockey League earned as much money as Jean was making with the Aces. The club paid him $7,000 in salary, the operators of the arena chipped in $5,000 more as their contribution to the pay of the star who was single-handedly filling their seats, and a soft-touch job as public relations man for a Quebec dairy netted him $3,000 more. In addition, there were other endorsements and public appearance fees that brought in another few thousand. Back home in Victoriaville, Arthur Beliveau long since had stopped protesting his eldest son's preoccupation with hockey. The six other Beliveau children were benefiting handsomely from Jean's success.

Phil Watson, the coach of the New York Rangers, had a coaching job in Quebec in those days, and he says the only way to describe it is to say that the whole city was in love with the tall, dark-haired hockey player. "For every goal he scored, he got a new suit," Watson says. "And he scored so many goals that he had enough suits left over to outfit every other man on the team. One of the best restaurants in town supplied him with all the steaks he could eat, free. They were glad just to have him come in the place. He could stay at any hotel in town for practically nothing. The people gave a big "night" for him and presented him with a brand-new automobile. He could park the car anywhere he wanted to and no policeman would even think of giving him a ticket. He had a radio program on which he promoted the sale of hockey sticks autographed by him, and he was a regular Arthur Godfrey when it came to drumming up business. The city loved him, that's all."

This was all very nice for Beliveau but more than a little bit hard on the officials of the Montreal Canadiens, who, year in and year out, were eating the dust of the powerful Detroit Red Wings. The Montreal fans couldn't understand why, if this Beliveau was half as good as the newspapers and the Quebec fans said he was, the Canadiens didn't put a major-league uniform on him and send him out on the floor of the historic Forum to show what he could do in competition with the best. If he could score 89 points in 57 games for the Aces, why couldn't he be a big help to the Canadiens in their fight to give Montreal the championship of the National Hockey League?

The answer, of course, was that Frank Selke, the man in the Canadiens' front office, knew he could, but Selke was up against a knotty financial problem. In 1952–53, the Aces drew 400,000 customers for their thirty home games, and the best estimates were that Beliveau's income from all sources was over $20,000. The only player in the National Hockey League earning that kind of money was Montreal's own Maurice Richard, and he was earning no more than that. Selke didn't have any enthusiasm for starting out even so spectacular a rookie as Beliveau at the same salary level as that achieved at the peak of a long career by the most exciting, the most successful and the most beloved player in the game. On the other hand, Beliveau was considerably less than enthusiastic about the idea of taking a salary cut to switch from amateur to professional hockey. The two were at loggerheads, and they remained that way until the Quebec Senior Hockey League, to which the Aces belonged, decided to change its status from amateur to professional.

This changed the picture considerably. The Canadiens still held that piece of paper giving them the rights to Beliveau's professional services. Jean had to play with the Canadiens or find another amateur team somewhere in the country willing to support him in the style to which he had become accustomed as a member of the Aces. Obviously, the second alternative was virtually impossible. No other amateur team in Canada could afford those prices because no other team had a huge arena and the kind of income that the Aces had. No matter how he looked at the problem, Jean had reached the point of having to go to work for the Canadiens. He still could bargain, however, and when he sat down at the table in Selke's office for his first serious contract discussion he was accompanied by his brother-in-law, who was the president of a substantial Montreal trust company, and by an income-tax expert. He was ready to do battle.

After an hour's negotiating, though, Jean grew tired of the haggling. "I want to play hockey," he said firmly. "Let's sign these papers and get it over with. The terms are all right." With no further fuss, he put his signature to a contract calling for approximately $100,000 in salary payments over a five-year period. According to insiders, he also received a $20,000 bonus for signing.

No hockey player in history ever came into the league on such a basis. The chances are none ever will again because it is hard to imagine a duplication of the special set of circumstances that existed in Beliveau's case.

The Montreal fans got their first look at the highly publicized rookie when he played three games with the Canadiens at the tail end of the 1952–53 season. The club didn't have any doubts about his ability but it seemed like a good idea to give him a thorough testing, and,

anyway, it would make the customers happy.
It made them almost delirious. Jean scored five
goals in the three games, coming up with three
goals in one game with the Rangers at the
Forum. Two of those goals were off passes to
him by Richard, and the Canadien rooters grew
dizzy with anticipation as they thought of what
their team would be able to do with these two
stars working together.

Dick Irwin, who was coaching the Canadiens
that year, said simply, "He's the best prospect
I've seen in twenty-five years." Nobody argued
with him.

Oddly enough, after his long war with the
club over wages, Jean played those three games
for no money at all. The customary payment
by a National Hockey League club to an amateur "trying out" on a short-term basis is a
hundred dollars per game, but, as Selke said,
it would have been an insult to offer a small
sum like that to a man who had helped draw almost 45,000 people to three games. Instead,
congratulating Jean on his engagement to Elise
Couture, a pretty, black-haired French-Canadian
girl whom he had met in Quebec, Selke told
him he wanted to buy them the finest furniture
they could find. Jean was happy to agree. In

June, 1953, he and Elise were married in St. Patrick's Church, Quebec. After they had built their own home a few years later, Jean collected his fee, and a handsome fee it was.

The Canadiens certainly never have regretted the money they spent to obtain Big Bill's services. When the gifted center joined a team that already had the magnificent Richard and the flamboyant Bernie (Boom Boom) Geoffrion, the Canadiens began to click, both at the box office and on the ice. Once the gang was welded into a smoothly functioning team, the Canadiens became the terrors of the league. They won championship after championship and they put on a show of hockey artistry that the oldest Canadians were willing to admit was the equal of anything the game ever had known.

Not that Jean tore the league apart from the very beginning. He didn't. For one thing, he suffered a couple of serious injuries. A split ankle bone kept him out of action for seven weeks, and he wasn't back in the lineup long before his cheekbone was broken. He ended up playing in only forty-four games and scoring a modest thirteen goals, a far cry from the thirty he had hoped to chalk up in his first year.

He was probably a little too individualistic after his five years as the whole show in Quebec, and it wasn't easy for him to blend into the more polished attack of the Canadiens. He was a little too deliberate, accustomed to taking his time about setting up his plays. He had been able to get away with that in the amateurs because nobody was able to give him any real opposition, but on the ice at the Forum he found a couple of hard-bitten pros piling into him unceremoniously every time he slowed up a notch and looked around to see what he ought to do next. They had no intention of letting him get set if they could help it. Jean learned, the hard way, that he had to go at top speed all the time and never ease up until the puck was safely in the net and the red light was blinking cheerfully to signal the score.

As his second season unfolded, it became clear that the rave notices Beliveau had attracted in Quebec had been nothing but the truth. He regained his confidence as he picked up the tricks of the professional trade. He let himself go, took chances the way he had done when he was the boss of the amateurs, and he wound up in a virtual dead heat with his teammates Geoffrion and Richard for the league scoring championship. It ended with Geoffrion posting 75 points, Richard 74 and Beliveau 73, a remarkable performance for a second-year player.

An added feather in Jean's cap that winter was his selection, along with Richard and defenseman Doug Harvey of the Canadiens, to the league's all-star team, an honor that is cherished by hockey players not only because of the prestige involved but because it carries with it a cash award of $1,000.

The only loose end left for him was the need to prove his toughness, and he didn't waste any time setting the record straight the following winter. With that hurdle cleared, there were no further doubts about him. The little flaws that had been exposed in his change-over to the pros, things like a split-second slowness on faceoffs and a tendency to keep the puck too long without passing it off to a teammate, were corrected so swiftly that now hockey people are prone to think back on Beliveau's first years as no different from today. It wasn't quite that easy for Jean, but it wasn't very hard, either. All he had to do was buckle down and make the most of his rare talent.

The parallel between Jean's hockey playing and the baseball playing of Joe DiMaggio was suggested to everybody by a poem that appeared in a Toronto newspaper. It wasn't exactly classic verse, but it made the point:

"For punch and color, it's the truth
Rocket Richard is hockey's Babe Ruth.
But what about this Beliveau?
He must be its DiMaggio."

Jean is a mature athlete now, enjoying his peak years. He has the satisfaction of playing on a team that is acknowledged to be one of the finest ever put together. He and Bert Olmstead and Bernie Geoffrion make up one offensive line, and Maurice Richard, his brother Henri and Dickie Moore make up another. There is work for all and glory for all. Perhaps Jean doesn't "own" Montreal the way he once owned Quebec—that could never happen, because the Rocket has a stranglehold on the innermost affections of the French-Canadians in Montreal—but he is both idolized and respected, and he is happy living there.

He plays baseball and golf for fun and for exercise in between hockey seasons, and he tries to make up for his failure to finish high school by reading a sizable hundred and fifty pages of classical literature every day. He loves to eat and has to watch his weight or he will find himself reporting to the Canadiens' training camp, as he did once, weighing closer to 230 pounds than to the 200 his coaches feel is his best playing weight. If he had no weight problem, Jean would surround his tender sirloin steaks with heaps of mashed potatoes and creamed vegetables, but except for holiday or other special dinners, he settles for green vegetables, lightly cooked, and mixed green salads. He knows what's good for him.

What's good for him is hockey, the slam-bang, incredibly fast, wildly exciting game that he can play better than any other man in the world.

Chapter Eight

CLEVELAND'S LEFT-HANDED FELLER, HERB SCORE

Herb Score's middle name is Jude; he took it as his confirmation name because he considers Saint Jude his patron saint.

You might wonder how a young man who has had so much misfortune in his life could feel that his patron saint has done a very good job of looking after him, but if you ask Herb about it, he has a ready answer. He refers you to the night of May 7, 1957, and the scene in Cleveland Municipal Stadium during the game between the Indians and the Yankees. It was a scene that shocked not only the thousands of fans seated in the stadium, but also the millions of people around the country who follow baseball with bated breath.

With two men out in the Yankees' half of the first inning of a scoreless ball game, Gil McDougald, playing shortstop for New York, smashed a line drive that struck Score in the right eye. As though he had been felled by an axe, Herb went down writhing on the ground. The first man who reached him was his roommate, Rocky Colavito, the right fielder. Rocky heard him say, "St. Jude, stay with me."

The ball had crashed squarely against the bone that protected Score's right eye. It had done some damage to the eye itself. "Luckily," said eye specialist Dr. Charles Thomas, "the ball struck him flush. It caught the top of the eyebrow bone, the cheekbone and the nose. The nose was fractured. It appears that the bone structure of his face absorbed most of the impact that would have destroyed his eye. There is no brain injury."

Everybody in baseball was worried that the accident might end Score's promising career. McDougald, the batter who had hit the ball, was quoted as saying that he was thinking of quitting the game if Herb was injured permanently. "This isn't worth it," McDougald told a reporter.

But St. Jude, whose medal Herb wears around his neck, must have been looking out for the young pitcher. Within a couple of days it had become apparent that Herb was going to be all right. "It just goes to prove," Herb says, "that St. Jude is the saint of hopeless cases, and I'm a hopeless case."

No matter how many jokes he made about it, though, Herb knew perfectly well that he had narrowly missed a crippling injury. Even as he was saying to Cleveland pitcher Mike Garcia, "You can't say I didn't keep my eye on that ball," Herb, lying on the ground near the pitcher's box, knew that he had been hurt badly. McDougald knew it, too, when he told reporters, "Right now, I'd a lot rather be up in that hospital room instead of Herb."

One of the last persons intimately concerned with the accident to hear about it was Herb's mother who lives in Lake Worth, Florida. She was shopping, and by the time she heard about the accident there was nothing anyone could do but pray. If God was willing, Herb would pitch again.

It wasn't the first time that Herb had depended upon divine help to carry him over a tough spot. His medical history shows an astonishing list of assorted injuries and illnesses that have plagued him since childhood. When he was only three years old, he was run over by a truck. Both of his legs were crushed only a few inches below the pelvis, and several doctors said that he would have to have his legs amputated if he hoped to live.

They were wrong, but a few months later, just as he was regaining the strength in his legs, he was put to bed with rheumatic fever.

In his freshman year in high school, he caught his toe on the gymnasium steps and fell, fracturing an ankle.

Even before the cast was removed from his ankle, he had to submit to an emergency appendicitis operation.

He has had two worrisome bouts with pneumonia and one with an agonizing colon condition.

He was rejected for military service because of high blood pressure.

He suffered a separation of his left shoulder in a fall in the outfield.

Nothing that had happened to him, of course, was anywhere near as bad as the shot in the eye that caromed off Gil McDougald's bat. But it didn't discourage Score. He refused even to concede that he might possibly be gun-shy at the plate in future games. "It's different with a batter who's been hit on the head by a pitched ball," Herb said. "I can understand his being afraid to stand up there. But not a pitcher. The only way he could show fear would be by refusing to throw the ball over the plate. I'm not going to do that. I have enough trouble getting the ball over as it is. I've been hit by line drives before, and I expect to get hit again, plenty of times. The one that caught me smack in the eye was a ten-million-to-one shot. Do you know anybody who's been hit by two ten-million-to-one shots? I don't either. I figure it happened, it's over, and I'm back at work."

Herb wasn't kidding, either. Some well-meaning advisors urged him to change his pitching style and avoid so complete a follow through. Then he would have no trouble following the return flight of the ball after it was hit. He flatly refused. "I'm not going to change my delivery," he said after he was released from the hospital. "I wouldn't be anywhere near as good a pitcher if I did. Lots of pitchers get hit by line drives, you know, but they usually get hit in the legs or the body. I just happened to get hit in the eye. It was a freak, that's all."

There is no question that Herb's deep religious faith had a great deal to do with carrying him through the difficult period after his accident. His sublime faith in his patron saint's watchfulness made him one hundred per cent certain that he would come back as good as ever.

Herb has been throwing with enthusiasm and accuracy since he was a small boy. In Rosedale, Long Island, New York, where he was born on June 7, 1933, Herb played the outfield and first base for Holy Name of Mary School until the coach, Father Thomas Kelly, notified him that he would be better off pitching. Father Kelly, an old Fordham shortstop, sensed that he could always get hold of an adequate outfielder or first baseman, but he would wait a long time for another pitcher like Herb Score. He threw him into the breach and promptly told him, "Herb, let's have no more of this outfield-first base nonsense. It won't surprise me if you make the big leagues some day."

After the family moved to Lake Worth, Florida, Herb pitched for the local high school until he became nineteen, and thus ineligible, in his senior year. By then, he already had come under the knowing eye of Cy Slapnicka, the famous Cleveland scout.

Slapnicka first was tipped off to Score's talent by a Lake Worth policeman, Tom Nagle. Cy made it his business to watch the boy in half a dozen high school ball games, and at the same time he took great pains to get to know Herb's family. When the boy became fair game for professional scouts, Slapnicka was so far ahead of the field that he didn't have to offer a sales talk in order to sign him to a Cleveland contract.

Not that there weren't other offers pressed upon the boy. The Chicago White Sox offered more money than the $60,000 the Indians paid, but Herb was unimpressed. "Neither my mother nor I felt that we ought to play one club against another," Herb says. "Somehow it didn't seem like the honest thing to do.

All the bids, including Cleveland's, were for so much more money than we'd ever known there was in the world that it didn't seem to make any difference which one I accepted." He freely admitted later on, though, that he had always had a feeling he would like best of all to sign with Cy Slapnicka, who knew all the important people and who could make the advent of the least impressive rookie look like the second coming of Joe DiMaggio. It was Slapnicka who had signed the great Bob Feller for Cleveland in 1936, and when Cy used the same kind of adjectives to describe Herb, people listened. Maybe, they thought, he was laying it on a bit, but then again, maybe not. He had done it once; why couldn't he do it again?

Slapnicka pulled no punches in making it clear that he was confident he *had* done it again. "He's pretty wild," the scout told a group of Cleveland newspapermen and club officials on a mild June day in 1952, "but he's fast. Man, what an arm! He's another Feller, only left-handed. He'll be the greatest." Feller himself later said, "Calling Herb Score a left-handed Feller is a great compliment to me."

After listening to that, everyone trooped out on the Cleveland Stadium field to watch 19-

year-old Herb show what he could do. Bill Lobe, the bullpen catcher, put on a mitt and settled himself to warm up the boy. The warm-up had scarcely begun when the ball exploded in Lobe's glove like a clap of thunder. Manager Al Lopez, Mel Harder, the pitching coach, and Red Ruffing, the old Yankee pitcher who works as a Cleveland trouble shooter now, looked both startled and alarmed. Ruffing reacted first. "Hey!" he called over to Score. "Take it easy, son! Wait'll your arm gets hot before you start cutting loose like that!"

Herb smiled back at Ruffing and said, "I'm not cutting loose, sir. I'm just throwing easy."

Slapnicka looked smug. "Stop worrying," he told the group. "He's just lobbing the ball. Wait till he lets go."

Within a few minutes, Herb let go, and the hard-bitten baseball men just stood there and stared. Other Cleveland ballplayers came up and watched. Herb was firing them in now, throwing bullets. As the players say, the ball whooshed into the plate so fast it looked like an aspirin tablet. "If he's going to pitch batting practice," one veteran said, "I just remembered I've got a stomach-ache. I'd better go lie down for a while."

Slapnicka got in the last word. "The kid can throw harder," he said, "but he's had a long train ride and he's a little tired."

The reporters in the crowd had a field day. They dusted off all their glowing phrases and heaped them on the slim blond boy's shoulders. They agreed that the bonus boy surely would have been put right to work in the American League if the Indians hadn't been so rich in pitchers, with men like Bob Lemon, Bob Feller, Early Wynn and Mike Garcia standing in line and elbowing each other for starting assignments. They predicted without hesitation that he would soon be the most valuable pitching property in the game.

Even the most enthusiastic sportswriter failed to envision the day that came in the spring of 1957 when Joe Cronin, the general manager of the Boston Red Sox, acting with the full approval of owner Tom Yawkey, offered a million dollars in cash for Herb Score's contract. The Indians, of course, had to turn down the bid; if they sold Score, they would be inviting their customers to stay home for good. But it was a breath-taking testimonial to the incalculable value of Herb's good left arm to a ball club fighting for the pennant.

Having made up their minds that it would be better to have Herb put in some time learning his trade before they turned him loose against the big-league hitters, the Cleveland officials wasted no time sending him to their top farm team, Indianapolis of the American Association. It was a compliment to Herb that they started him out so high. As it turned out, he wasn't quite ready for it. He was tremendously fast, all right, but he was also fearfully wild and almost totally lacking in knowledge of the little tricks of the trade. He won only two games at Indianapolis, losing five, and although he struck out sixty-one batters in the sixty-two innings he pitched, he also managed to walk sixty-two.

For the 1953 season, he was placed with the Reading, Pennsylvania, club in the Eastern League, several notches below Indianapolis. His won-and-lost record improved somewhat as he chalked up seven victories against only three defeats, but he was still wild. In 98 innings of pitching, he gave up the staggering total of 126 bases on balls, an average of almost 12 walks per nine-inning game. ("We used to hate to see Herb go out to pitch," one of his old Reading teammates said. "We knew he'd walk everybody but the peanut vendor and we'd be out there for three and a half hours.") They don't let anyone pitch in the major leagues who has that much trouble finding the plate, and for the first time the men back in Cleveland Stadium began to wonder if their jewel in the rough was going to turn out to be one of those precious stones which nobody can polish for commercial use.

Then, all of a sudden, in 1954, back in Indianapolis, Herb's astonishing natural power was harnessed to skill and control. He came under the instruction of Ted Wilks, the old St. Louis Cardinal relief pitcher, who corrected the flaws in Herb's delivery. Everything went right for him. He won 22 games and lost only 5, but, most exciting of all, he piled up 330 strike-outs against only 140 bases on balls in 251 innings of pitching. He was ready for the big league, and that's where he went. The chances are that he will stay there for a long time.

In addition to talent, Herb brings boundless energy and ambition to his job as a major-league pitcher. He keeps himself in perfect condition; he neither drinks nor smokes. He works furiously at the ball park and listens patiently and thoughtfully to every piece of advice given him by his manager and coaches and the older, more experienced ballplayers. He wants to get ahead, he wants to become the great pitcher that everybody has been telling him he can be, and he doesn't intend to trust to luck. He is willing to work for it.

Herb has always been grateful that he came up to the Indians in 1955 along with his roommate and closest friend at Reading and Indianapolis, Rocky Colavito. Rocky, who has established himself as the club's leading slugger, is a Bronx, New York boy who was raised in the shadow of Yankee Stadium and eats, sleeps and dreams baseball. He and Herb are the same age and they share a lot of common interests, especially listening to jazz and "country style" records, and eating Italian-style cooking. Furthermore, both are devout Catholics and go to church together when the club is on the road. Ever since their rookie days in Reading, they have made a habit of praying for each other's success.

Sometimes a fan in the stands will see one or both of the boys make the sign of the cross before a ball game and will write to complain that such religious expressions have no part in baseball. Both Herb and Rocky always take pains to answer such letters, asking the fan, "What's wrong with having faith?"

A few of the letters, of course, are especially hard to take. "What good did your prayers do you that time, you phony?" one cynic wrote after Herb had lost a tough ball game. "People like that," he says, "never sign their names. I wish they would. I'd especially like to answer them, just to explain that I never pray simply to be allowed to win a ball game or to strike out a dozen hitters. I'd be a praying man if I was a ditchdigger."

He would also be a terrific ditchdigger because Herb Score believes in giving everything he has to what he is doing. Even when he was going so badly at Reading, he put his heart and soul into every game. And when he wasn't pitching, he was practicing. It was no accident that his talent reached maturity the next year at Indianapolis and that he became a winning pitcher his first season with the Indians.

Herb won't ever forget his first start for Cleveland. It was the second game of the 1955 season. The Indians were playing at Detroit, and it was a raw, cold April day. There were only 3,786 people in the stands at Briggs Stadium, but they sounded like a lot to Herb

Score as he listened to them yelling for the Tiger batters to knock the ball out of the park. They didn't quite do that, but they did rough him up a good deal right from the start. Harvey Kuenn and Fred Hatfield reached him for singles and the young slugger, Al Kaline, drove in a run with a long fly ball. Herb managed to get out of the inning without further difficulty, but he found himself in hot water in the second when he loaded the bases on three walks. He got out of that one by striking out his opposing pitcher, Frank Lary, but by now, despite the chill in the air, he was sweating.

It took him four innings to settle down. He had been so afraid of walking everybody that he had been taking too careful aim at the plate and had been holding back on his fast ball. As his confidence returned, he began to wind up in the loose, easy manner that was natural to him, and the fast ball began to smack into the catcher's mitt with the old, satisfying sound. His curve was breaking the way it ought to break, and the Tigers were beginning to realize that this nice-looking young kid was going to be hard to handle. It was a tough ball game until the eighth inning when the Indians put

on a burst of power and went into a 7–2 lead.
Herb gave up one more run before it was
over, but he had won his first major-league
victory in convincing fashion and he felt he
had proved that he belonged.

If there were any lingering doubts in anyone's mind, they were chased away on Sunday, May 1, when the one and only, the original Bob Feller, and his left-handed carbon
copy teamed up to overwhelm the Boston Red
Sox in a double-header. Feller threw a one-
hitter, the twelfth of his great career, against
the Red Sox in the first game. In the second
game, Herb served notice on the whole American League that he had come into his own. He
struck out a whopping sixteen men—only two
fewer than Feller's all-time record of eighteen
strike-outs for a single game—and gave only
four hits in beating the Red Sox, 2–1. Nine of
his strike-outs came in the first three innings.
The eye-catching performance made him a
member of a select group of eight pitchers
who had struck out sixteen or more batters in
a nine-inning game. (Feller had done it three
times.)

After it was all over, and the Indians were
getting dressed, the reporters descended upon

the Cleveland locker room to fire questions at Herb. Feller, whose amazing feat in the first game had set the tone for the day's pitching fireworks, already had gone home. For the first time in his young life, Herb Score had to face the crowd of interviewers alone.

"That sixth inning hurt you," one writer said. "If they hadn't got that double play, you might have come up with another strike-out."

"Nothing hurt me," Herb said evenly. "I was just trying to get the side out. That double play looked mighty good to me."

"Weren't you disappointed that you didn't break the strike-out record?" another writer wanted to know.

"Heck, no," Herb said. "I'm glad I finished the game, and I'm glad I won it."

Al Lopez, the manager, supplied the last word as the reporters were on their way out. "Isn't he a nice boy?" he said. Nobody contradicted him.

It was a fine year for Herb. He went on to win sixteen games and lose ten, a remarkable record for an inexperienced pitcher. The 245 strike-outs he hung up set a new major-league record for a first-year pitcher. Not only was he winning ball games for the Indians, but, as

Feller had in his prime, he was pulling customers in at the gate. Sports fans relish, more
than anything else, the decisive skill. They go
for the fighter who packs a knock-out punch,
for the hitter who knocks home runs soaring
out of the park, for the football player with
a knack for reeling off seventy-yard runs, and
for the pitcher with the strike-out touch. They
loved Herb Score, and they turned out in
great numbers to watch him pitch. When he
followed up his fine freshman year with a bril-
liant 20-victory season in 1956, and put 263
more strike-outs in the record book, they put
aside any hesitation and loudly proclaimed him
one of the all-time greats.

It is Herb Score's cross that his physical
troubles have kept him from living up to the
promise of those first two seasons. Not that
anybody doubts his ability to pitch as effec-
tively as ever; when he is healthy, he proves
that he can. But ever since the night Gil
McDougald's line drive smashed him in the
eye, he has known nothing but trouble. His
record for 1957 was a pitiful two victories and
one defeat. Virtually the whole season was devoted to recuperating from the shocking injury that came so near to ending his career.

Many a baseball man soberly believed that Herb never would be able to pitch again.

In July Herb had married his long-time sweetheart, Nancy McNamara, after her graduation from St. Mary's College in South Bend, Indiana. After he returned to Cleveland from his honeymoon he began light workouts, and in a few weeks he had regained the full strength of his muscular arms and legs. The trouble was that he couldn't focus his damaged eye on the ball. Standing on the pitcher's mound, sixty feet from home plate, he couldn't see the catcher. It was then that more than one of the Cleveland officials privately gave up on him. They didn't think he would ever be able to come back. Surely, they felt, he would never be the same.

But neither Herb nor Dr. Charles I. Thomas, the eye specialist who took care of him, ever gave up hope. At first, they were the only ones who thought they detected any improvement, but they stayed firm in their faith. When the ball club disbanded for the fall and winter, Herb began a schedule of planned exercises designed to bring him up to spring training in top shape. By the time he walked out on the practice field at Tucson, Arizona, in March, he knew he was all right. The only question that remained to be answered was whether or not his frightening experience had made him gun-shy, afraid of the batted ball. As soon as his buddy, Rocky, showed up in camp, Herb set about finding out once and for all. He made Rocky dig in at the plate and swing full force at his pitches. When he thought Rocky was deliberately trying to hit the ball to the sides of the field, away from him, Herb called a halt and laid down the law. "Come on," he said, "this isn't doing me any good. You get a cigar if you can hit me in the teeth."

Of course, the skeptics weren't going to be convinced until they saw how Herb handled himself under full combat conditions. The answer came late in March during an exhibition game with the Chicago Cubs. With two out in the second inning, rookie third-baseman John Goryl of the Cubs slashed a hot one-bouncer right at Herb's head. Casually, as though it were the most routine play in the world, Herb picked the ball off with his gloved hand and threw Goryl out at first. The Indians finally knew that Herb not only could see the ball, he could handle it, too. His faith had seen him through, just as he had known it would.

Unhappily, the bad luck that has plagued him through one mishap after another didn't leave him in 1958. A wickedly inflamed elbow that absolutely refused to clear up kept Herb on the side lines for most of the season. Persistent flare-ups of the trouble caused the club to place him on the disabled list on July 15, and he didn't throw a ball again for over a month. For the second year in a row, he finished the season charged with no responsibility except to get ready for next year.

Twenty-five years old, Herb has seen two full seasons go down the drain at a time when he had hoped to be approaching his peak. A less determined, more easily shaken man might have given in to the worry that he was "jinxed." But not Herb. He remembers the time when he was pitching for Indianapolis and had a no-hitter going against the Kansas City Blues with two out in the ninth inning and two strikes on the batter, Art Schult. Looking for the third strike, he broke off a sharp curve that catcher Hank Foiles thought sure was the game-ending pitch. When the umpire called it a ball, Foiles jumped up and down behind the plate and argued hotly that it was a clean strike. The umpire didn't see it that way, and Foiles came close to being thrown out of the game. When he finally settled down, Herb wound up and came in with another fast pitch. Schult drove it on a line right out of the park. In the clubhouse, Foiles was beside himself with rage, but Herb calmed him down. "Forget it, Hank," he said. "When God wants us to have a no-hitter, we'll get it."

That's the way Herbert Jude Score feels today. He has no complaints about anything. God, he knows, gave him the ability to pitch strikes to major-league hitters; God protected him when that line drive smashed into his face and almost blinded him; and God will give him back his strength and his health in good time.

When the time comes, the American League had better watch out. Herb has a lot of lost time to make up.

VISION BOOKS

All Vision Books have full color jackets, black and white illustrations, sturdy full cloth bindings. Imprimatur.